Catholicism

for

Protestants

Shane Schaetzel

Regnum Dei Press

RegnumDeiPress.com

2013

Nihil Obstat: **Reverend Allan Saunders, Censor Librorum**
Imprimatur: **Most Reverend James V. Johnston, Jr., D.D., J.C.L.**
Bishop of Springfield-Cape Girardeau, September 6, 2013

The nihil obstat and imprimatur are declarations that a book or pamphlet is free of doctrinal or moral error. No implication is contained therein that those who have granted the nihil obstat or imprimatur agree with the contents, opinions or statements expressed.

To my family:
Penny, Michael & Lauren

May they never be timid
to proclaim their faith.

CONTENTS

FOREWORD

By Father Christopher Phillips

I love Protestants. For one thing, I have to – I come from a long line of them. Some of my earliest and fondest memories come from my experiences at the little Methodist Church in the town where I grew up. In fact, my father has told the story frequently of how I got my first spanking in church – and with some satisfaction would end it by saying, "It must've worked... never had to spank him again."

Mingled with those early memories is a particular one that comes from my early teen-age years. Our youth group leader decided it would be a good experience for us to visit other churches. We went to all the usual places – Episcopalian, Congregational, Baptist – all the standard places within reasonable distance. But he put off the most difficult until last; namely, the local Catholic Church. It was somewhat controversial that we'd even consider visiting a Catholic Church. After all, I can remember one of my Sunday School teachers telling us, "There are Christians and then there are Catholics." She didn't mean to imply that Catholics were necessarily bad people – it's just that they weren't Christians, at least by our reckoning. Even the name of the place was strange to our ears: "Immaculate Conception Catholic Church." To me, it didn't have the same ring as "First Baptist" or "Central Congregational" or even our own Methodist Church which was named after our little town, Bakerville. I mean, what was an "Immaculate Conception" and why would it be the name of a church? It struck me as being pretty exotic.

I still remember the visit like it was last week. It seemed like everyone was bobbing up and down, and kneeling at the oddest times (something we didn't do in the Methodist Church, except when we received the bread and Welch's grape juice at Communion on the first Sunday of every quarter-year). I spent most of the time looking from side to side, trying to figure out what was going on. That is, except for the time that I stared straight ahead at what seemed to me to be the biggest statue I had ever seen. I didn't know who it was supposed to be, but I figured she must be somebody pretty important. Anyway, it all seemed fairly confusing to me, and when we left I can remember thinking to myself, "I'm never coming back to this place!"

Actually, I did return about twenty-five years later. I was living in Texas, and was making a visit to my home town in Connecticut where my extended family still lived. I returned to Immaculate Conception Church once again – but this time as a Catholic priest. How in the world could such a thing have happened? It happened because I learned what you are about to learn in the pages of this book.

I've been a Catholic priest for thirty years, and in that time I have worked with countless people, mostly Protestants, who have expressed a mixture of curiosity and interest in the Catholic Church. Most frequently in these conversations a statement would be made which goes something like this: "I'm sorry, but I just can't accept what you Catholics believe about..." (and here you can insert any number of things, like papal infallibility, the Immaculate Conception, the Assumption of Mary – the list could go on). My response is always this: "Tell me what you think we believe about that." Almost invariably, by the time they finish, I can honestly tell them, "If the Church taught that, I wouldn't accept it either!"

I wish this book had been available thirty years ago. How great it would have been, after having a conversation with someone about the Catholic faith, if I could have given them a copy of this as a further help to their understanding. In fact, I wish I'd had this book fifty years ago, when I was a confused youngster, ready to write off two thousand years of Catholic faith!

Of course, we shouldn't fool ourselves. There are real doctrinal differences to be contended with – differences among the various Protestant denominations themselves, and also between Protestants generally and the Catholic Church. Those are things for the professional theologians and commissions to work on. But so much of what keeps the average Protestant wary about Catholicism is due to simple misunderstanding and the lack of a clear presentation of the traditional and historic Catholic faith.

Shane Schaetzel has done a great service to Protestants and Catholics alike by presenting Catholic truth clearly and simply through a series of questions and answers. The questions are those which are asked frequently by Protestants; the answers are straight out of the deep richness of Catholic teaching. In fact, reflected in these pages is one of the things I love most about Catholicism; its profound simplicity. Simple enough to be understood by a child, but so profound that even the most brilliant people are brought to their knees.

May God's blessing be upon you as you read these pages. Invite the Lord Jesus Christ to be your companion as you learn, and may the Holy Ghost increase your love for the Truth.

Fr. Christopher G. Phillips
Pastor, Our Lady of the Atonement Church
San Antonio, Texas

CHAPTER ONE
INTRODUCTION

Roman Catholics living in the Ozark Mountains of Southern Missouri and Northern Arkansas, know full well what it is like to be a minority religion in the "Bible Belt" of the United States. Since most people in this part of America are of Baptist, Pentecostal and Evangelical belief, they often don't have much knowledge of what Catholicism really is, or what Catholics really believe. They may even have some misunderstandings. This book is in a Question and Answer format, designed specifically for people in this area, or anyone else who might have a similar curiosity. I will intentionally try to keep the answer to each question as brief as I possibly can for this purpose, yet still be detailed enough so as to give a respectable explanation. The following is a compilation of real questions I have actually received from real people here in the Ozark Mountains of Southern Missouri and Northern Arkansas.

The reader may notice an unusual characteristic in the spelling within this book. That's because I typically use U.K. spelling, even though I am an American with a profound U.S. syntax. I originally started using U.K. spelling when I began blogging in the summer of 2012. I noticed that it helped generate more of an international audience, and I liked the way it looked on paper. So in these pages you will find a usage of English that was quite common in the Southern American states in previous centuries, but not so much in recent decades. It's U.K. spelling with U.S. syntax. Hopefully, the reader will not find this too terribly distracting.

The reader may take note of my liberal usage of the word "Protestant" in this book. Indeed the title itself will probably raise a few eyebrows. I am quite aware that some Evangelical Christians object to usage of this word in reference to them. I assure the reader that when I use the word "Protestant," there is no ill intent. It is simply a classification, much in the same way the word "Catholic" is a classification. There are many different kinds of Catholics. There are: Roman Catholics, Byzantine Catholics, Maronite Catholics, Franciscans, Benedictines, Carmelites, and even Anglican Use Catholics. Yet they are all Catholics in union with Rome and under the authority of the pope. The same goes for Protestants. There are many different kinds: Anglican, Lutheran, Methodist, Presbyterian, Baptist, Pentecostal, Evangelical and those who simply wish to be called "born again Christians." Yet they are all Protestants in a general sense, in that their spiritual roots can be easily traced back to the sixteenth century Protestant Reformation. Traditionally, the word "Protestant" has been used for mainline traditional denominations (Anglican, Lutheran, Methodist, Reformed, etc.); while Christians outside these denominations have been referred to under the general term "Evangelical." For the purpose of this book, they are all classified simply as "Protestant."

The reader may also notice that the majority of the questions contained herein deal primarily with Baptist, Pentecostal and Evangelical concerns. Whereas, traditional Protestants might not have the same concerns. Here in the Bible Belt of the United States, the overwhelming vast majority of Protestants are: Baptist, Pentecostal and Evangelical. Demographic analysis over the last thirty years has shown that these groups now make up the majority of Protestants, both in the United States, and around the world. They are also growing at such an exponential rate, that it is only a matter of time before they completely dominate the entire Protestant ethos. At this present rate, within less than a generation, these groups will represent the overwhelming vast majority of all Protestantism. Oh sure, mainline traditional denominations are not going away anytime soon. They have enough resources to hang on for a good long time, but in comparison to Evangelical and Pentecostal groups, their rate of growth is very modest, and in some cases, even regressive. Therefore, the majority of questions Catholics deal with in the Bible Belt, will soon be the majority of questions all Catholics will deal with wherever Protestants are numerous. Thus, the questions addressed in this book should become increasingly more relevant worldwide as time progresses.

At this point, a little background information is probably in order. I am a Roman Catholic layman of the Anglican Use and a fourth degree Knight of Columbus, but this was not always the case. I was actually baptised in the Missouri Synod of the Lutheran Church shortly after my birth in Southern California. My father was Lutheran, and comes from a long line of Lutherans stretching back to the sixteenth century. My mother was raised Southern Baptist in Western Tennessee. As a compromise, my parents raised my sisters and I in the American Baptist Church (Northern Baptist) which held to Baptist doctrine but was a bit more liturgical in practise. Upon reaching adulthood I branched out on my own, looking for the Church I believed had the most continuity with early Christianity. I eventually settled on an Evangelical nondenominational church where I met Penny, the woman who would eventually become my wife. Penny was baptised Methodist, but was raised in a variety of religious traditions. Together we remained Evangelicals while I studied for the ministry.

It was through these studies that I discovered the Jewish roots of the Christian faith and the writings of the early Church fathers. You'll notice I cite these writings throughout this book, both by quotation and footnote. This is because in order to understand what early Christians believed and practiced, we need to read what they left behind for us in their writings. The early Christians were prolific writers for their time, and they have left for us a rather detailed record. From these writings, combined with the sacred Scriptures, we can reconstruct a fairly accurate image of what the early Church was like. In these writings, I found a continuity with ancient Judaism of course, but I also discovered them to be much more "catholic" than I was comfortable with. My understanding of Christian doctrine began to change with this, and in time, I could no longer preach what I truly believed on Sunday mornings when I filled in for the head pastor. At this point, Penny and I quietly left our Evangelical church and began looking for a place where we could familiarise ourselves with catholic traditions in what we believed to be a "good, safe, Protestant environment." We eventually settled down as Anglicans in a moderately conservative Episcopal Church.

We loved this little Episcopal Church, we loved its priest, and we particularly loved the liturgy of the Anglican tradition. It seemed to solve a great deal of problems for us, and we would have stayed there were it not for the overtly progressive direction of the national denomination. We looked into more conservative Anglican alternatives, but at that time, our area did not have any of reasonable size. Penny felt uncomfortable moving to a smaller church and wanted something larger if we were no longer going to stay with the Episcopal Church. It was at this point I knew we had to make a choice between Roman Catholicism or Eastern Orthodoxy.

So I seriously began looking into the doctrines of both institutions and compared them with the teachings of the early Christian Church. Both Catholicism and Orthodoxy were very appealing for similar reasons, but in the end, it all came down to the issue of Christian authority. We chose the Roman Catholic Church and received the sacraments of Confirmation and Holy Eucharist at Saint Elizabeth Ann Seton Church in Springfield Missouri, on the 22nd day of April, in the year of our Lord 2000. It was the Easter Vigil. Since then we have been blessed with two children and both were baptised as Roman Catholics.

I have dedicated this book to my family, who I hope will never take their Catholic Christian faith for granted, nor be embarrassed to call themselves Catholic. For sometimes, when other Christians are quick to judge or discriminate because of our Catholicism, it is easy to give up and try to blend in. May this never be the case. We Catholics are very Biblical Christians, and I hope this book will effectively demonstrate that.

CHAPTER TWO
GENERAL QUESTIONS

QUESTION: Are Catholics Christians?

ANSWER: Yes, Catholics are not only Christians, but we were the first Christians. The Roman Catholic Church is the oldest Christian Church founded by Jesus Christ in 33 AD, and planted in Rome in about 42 AD,[1] when Saint Peter established his apostolic see in Rome after planting a church in Antioch.[2] Peter was later crucified in Rome, upside down, in the year 67 AD.[3] His direct successors became the popes.

QUESTION: Do Catholics believe in Jesus Christ?

ANSWER: Yes, of course we believe in Jesus Christ. We believe he is God the Son – the Second Person of the Holy Trinity (Father, Son and Holy Spirit) – made flesh and blood, taking on a fully human form, and becoming fully man in every way, yet retaining his full divinity.[4] We believe in his life, virgin birth, miracles, ministry, suffering, death and resurrection. We also believe he is currently reigning as the King of kings in Heaven, and he will one day return to judge the living and the dead.[5]

QUESTION: What do Catholics mean by the Holy Trinity?

---

1 Irenaeus, Against Heresies, 3:1:1 (circa 180 AD); Eusebius of Caesarea, The Chronicle (circa 303 AD)

2 Clement of Rome, The First Epistle of Clement, 5 (circa 96 AD); Irenaeus, Against Heresies, 3:1:1 (circa 180 AD); Eusebius, Church History, 2:14,5 (circa 325 AD)

3 Gauss, fragment in Eusebius' Church History, 2:25 (circa 198 AD); Tertian, Against Marcion, 4:5 (circa 210 AD); Tertullian, Scorpiace,15:3 (circa 212 AD); Peter of Alexandria, The Canonical Epistle, Canon 9 (circa 306 AD); Cyril of Jerusalem, Catechetical Lectures, 6:14-15 (circa 350 AD)

4 Catechism of the Catholic Church; paragraphs 464 - 470, 480 - 482

5 Catechism of the Catholic Church; pages 56 - 57

ANSWER: We believe in ONE God, who is eternally existent in three divine Persons: Father, Son and Holy Spirit.[6] This is the teaching of the Holy Scriptures (Matthew 3:16-17; Matthew 28:19; John 1:1; John 8:59-59; John 10:30-33; John 14:26; John 15:26; John 20:28; 2nd Corinthians 13:14; Galatians 4:4-6; Titus 2:13) and the early Church. The first Christians gave their lives for this faith. As Justin Martyr wrote in 155 AD: *"Our teacher of these things is Jesus Christ, who also was born for this purpose, and was crucified under Pontius Pilate, procurator of Judaea, in the times of Tiberius Caesar; and that we reasonably worship Him, having learned that He is the Son of the true God Himself, and holding Him in the second place, and the prophetic Spirit in the third, we will prove."* – (Justin Martyr, First Apology 13)

The doctrine of the Trinity was taught from the earliest days of the Church, and it is helpful to remember that the people who gave their lives as martyrs in the Roman circuses (made into human torches and lion food) died believing that Jesus Christ is God, and that he is the second Person of the Holy Trinity. The name "Trinity" was used as early as the third century to briefly describe the triune nature of God. The doctrine was finally defined dogmatically in the early fourth century at the Council of Nicea in response to the Arian heresy.[7] Thus the Catholic Christian faith was dogmatically defined as those Christians who maintained belief in the Trinity, as opposed to those Christians who followed Arius in denying the Trinity.

The doctrine of the Trinity is universally accepted by all Christian churches that broke with the Catholic Church in the sixteenth century and thereafter. It is taught by all Christian

---

6 Catechism of the Catholic Church; paragraphs 232, 234, 237, 261 & 266

7 Arian heresy: In the early fourth century a rogue priest named Arius introduced the teaching that Jesus Christ is not divine and that God is not a Trinity. This caused such a great disturbance in the early Church that an ecumenical council was called in the City of Nicea (located in Asia Minor) in which all of the bishops were summoned to investigate this matter. They condemned the Arian heresy, affirmed the Trinity as the universal faith taught by the apostles, formulated the Nicene Creed, and ordered the compilation of a universal New Testament to combat this heresy.

churches connected to the Catholic Church through history and baptism. It is the universal doctrine of all Protestant denominations: Lutheran, Anglican, Methodist, Reformed, Presbyterian, Baptist, Pentecostal, Evangelical and many more. Christianity has always been defined as a Trinitarian faith, meaning the belief in ONE God in three equally divine Persons. There are of course some churches that no longer teach the Trinity. These churches are no longer connected to the Catholic Church either through history or baptism. For that matter, they are no longer connected to Protestantism either, and most of them have no problem telling you that.

QUESTION: Is Catholicism a cult?

ANSWER: This is a fun question. When some Protestants call Catholicism a "cult," there has never been a better example of the proverbial *pot calling the kettle "black!"* Religions are defined by their definition of God. If Catholicism is a "cult" then so is every Protestant denomination and affiliation, as they all subscribe to the same Catholic doctrine of the Holy Trinity and belief that Jesus Christ is God.

Protestants are connected to Catholicism both through history and baptism. They are essentially catholics (with a small "c") because, unlike some churches that also use the name Christian,[8] Protestant churches accept the Trinity, as well as other distinctively Catholic traits. However, these functionally catholic Christians actively *protest* various teachings and practises of the Roman Catholic Church, hence the name *Protest*ant. Some Protestants prefer to be called Reformed, Evangelical or "born again" Christians. Others just prefer be labeled according to their denomination. (The term "Protestant" itself is simply a descriptive way to refer to all of them and is in no way intended as a pejorative

---

8 These include; Jehovah's Witness, Christian Science, and the Church of Jesus Christ of Latter Day Saints, just to name a few.

in this book.) They all accept the Trinitarian definition of God. They worship Jesus Christ as God the Son. They use a New Testament that was compiled and canonised by the Catholic Church sixteen-hundred years ago (see Chapter 4). They celebrate Christian feasts (Christmas, Easter, All Hallows Eve, Saint Patrick's Day & Saint Valentine's Day) according to the Roman Catholic liturgical calendar.[9] They follow the Catholic practise of worshipping on Sundays. They arrange their churches with pews, an elevated sanctuary and occasionally an altar. All of these are essentially Roman Catholic traits. They've even retained some traditional Catholic hymns in some cases. What makes them different is their rejection of Roman Catholic authority, and some Roman Catholic traditions, which they pick and choose as they see fit. Some Protestants, like the Anglicans for example, follow Catholic tradition quite closely, minus full submission to the authority of the pope of course. Other Protestants, like Seventh Day Adventists[10] for example, reject just about every Catholic tradition they can, including worship on Sundays. Most other Protestant denominations fall somewhere in between. If Catholicism is a "cult," than so is every Protestant church in the world.

No, Catholicism is not a "cult." We believe in the same God as Protestants and we don't engage in cult-like methods of deception and mind control. The Catholic Church is very transparent about its teachings and what it expects of its members.

QUESTION: Are Catholics "saved" or "born again?"

---

9 Eastern Christians use a completely different liturgical calendar, marking different dates for Christmas and Easter, as well as different Saint days. While Protestants continue to cling to the Western calendar, formulated by the Roman Catholic Church, for the celebration of these holidays.

10 Contrary to popular belief, the Seventh Day Adventists still accept the doctrine of the Trinity and the divinity of Jesus Christ, in spite of their affinity toward Sabbath keeping. So while many SDA Christians have a very negative opinion of the Catholic Church, they still cling to core Trinitarian catholic dogma.

ANSWER: Yes. However, we Catholic Christians don't look at this as a one-time event like many "born-again" Christians or Evangelicals. While we believe we are "born again" through baptism (John 3:2-5),[11] which is the Biblical context of the saying "born again," we also believe in salvation as an ongoing process that is past, present and future. Yes, I *was* saved (Romans 8:24) at my baptism. Yes, I *am being* saved (Philippians 2:12) as I live my life in Christ. Yes, I believe I *will be* saved (Matthew 10:22) upon my death and when Christ returns. Catholics don't usually do one-time "altar calls" wherein the pastor asks people to come to the front of the chapel, say the "sinner's prayer" and publicly "give their hearts to Jesus Christ." Rather, Catholics are asked to do the same thing every week by reception of the sacraments. When one receives the sacrament of the Holy Eucharist (Greek: "Thanksgiving") in Communion, one is asked to receive Jesus Christ. The same holds true with the sacrament of penance, wherein one says something similar to the sinner's prayer, as well as the other sacraments wherein Catholics rededicate their lives to Christ. For Catholics, "giving one's heart to Jesus Christ" is an ongoing process that never ends.

QUESTION: Do some Catholic practises have Pagan origin?

ANSWER: This is highly unlikely even though that accusation has been repeatedly made by some Protestants over the last two centuries. In fact, it has been said so much, by so many different people, that it is often just accepted as "fact," even by some Catholics! Many of the so-called "Pagan" practises of Catholicism actually come from ancient Judaism, not Paganism, and in particular the Temple ceremonies of the ancient Jewish religion, coupled with common synagogue practises from the first century.

For example, the Catholic burning of incense is sometimes thought to be of Pagan origin, but it was actually a common

---

11 Catechism of the Catholic Church; paragraphs 1212, 1215 - 1216

practise in the Jewish Temple period and commanded by God (Exodus 30:8). This custom was transferred to the New Testament era in St. John's revelation of pure Heavenly worship (Revelation 5:8). Thus in imitation of pure Heavenly worship, and the ancient Jewish worship of God, Catholic priests will typically burn incense around the altar within a Catholic church.

Another common accusation is that Sunday was used to worship the Pagan sun idol. Thus, it is said, Catholics transferred worship from Saturday (Sabbath) to Sunday so as to accommodate Pagan converts from this religion. Actually, that is false. The institution of Sunday as the designated Christian day of worship was put into place by the apostles (Acts 20:7) and was called the "Lord's Day" (Revelation 1:10). This was done in recognition of Jesus' resurrection on a Sunday, or the "*first day of the week*" – (John 20:1).

Yet another extremely common accusation is that the celebration of Christmas comes from the Pagan feast of the winter solstice and that the Catholic Church simply absorbed this practise to again accommodate ancient sun worshippers. These accusations seem to have originated in the middle nineteenth century and offer no definitive proof of their validity. Most history scholars have now debunked the "Pagan origin theory" of Christmas even though it is still widely accepted by the general population. A deeper investigation into the ancient Roman sun cult revealed that its holiest day was on August 9th, and that Roman sun worshippers ironically did not observe the equinoxes and solstices. On the other hand, two other things were going on at that time.

First, the Roman Jews, who followed Jesus as the Messiah, were put out of the synagogues (excommunicated from Judaism) in the late first century. Thus they no longer had access to the Jewish calendar. The Jewish feast of Hanukkah always fell on the 25th day of the Jewish month of Kislev. However, without access to that calendar or the synagogue, it became difficult to calculate the proper day for this celebration which had great cultural significance to Jewish people. This was especially true for Jewish Christians, who commemorated Jesus' celebration of the feast recorded in John 10:22-23. Since the Jewish month of Kislev most commonly overlaps with the Julian month of December, it is believed many of these Jewish Christians in Rome celebrated their Christianised version of Hanukkah on December 25th instead, which usually falls close to Kislev 25th. Just as regular Jews celebrated the light that came into the Temple during this feast, so Christian Jews in Rome celebrated Jesus, the Light of God, who came into the same Temple during this feast. This Jewish-Christian Hanukkah being an eight-day festival, with its conclusion on January 1st, eventually came to be known as the "Christmas Octave", on the Roman Catholic liturgical calendar.

Second, December 25th later came to be associated with the birth of Christ due to an earlier commemoration of his conception. This Feast of the Annunciation came to be celebrated on March 25th (which also came from another, completely different, Jewish custom),[12] that is exactly nine months before December 25th. Now all of this is just liturgical commemoration. I don't know anybody who really believes Jesus was actually born on December 25th, and I am not aware of any Church doctrine that insists that he was. (Still, that doesn't stop some groups from using this as a straw-man to attack the Catholic Church's celebration of Christmas.) As ancient Christians in Rome increasingly marked December 25th as a holy day, the Pagan Roman emperor created the Feast of Sol Invictus (The Unconquered Sun) on December 25th in 274 AD. He allegedly did this in an attempt to unite Christians and Pagans in the empire under a common date for their religious celebrations. If indeed that was his intention, it turned out to be a miserable failure,

---

12 Integral Age: An ancient Jewish custom wherein it was believed that great prophets were conceived or born on the same date as their death. Since at that time it was believed that Jesus died on March 25th (according to the Julian calendar), that date came to be associated with his conception as well.

as both *Sol Invictus*, and the Roman sun cult, died out within a couple centuries.

No, it is not Catholicism that adopted Pagan dates and practices, but rather it is much more likely the other way around. The evidence seems to suggest that it was the Pagans, who in the twilight of their glory days, desperately tried to adopt Christian dates and practises to revive their dying religions. There are, of course, many more false accusations of crypto-Paganism within the Catholic Church, but the above demonstrates that these can be easily refuted with a little knowledge of history, religion and culture.

QUESTION: Must a person understand Latin to be a Catholic?

ANSWER: No. While Latin is the historical language of the Roman Catholic Church in the Western world, and it is helpful to know a little Latin, it is by no means required. While the Church has always retained its celebration of the ancient Latin liturgy,[13] it has in recent decades translated all of its liturgies into many vernacular translations. Today, people should have no problem finding a liturgy celebrated in their own spoken language.

QUESTION: Is the Catholic Church opposed to modern science?

ANSWER: No. Quite to the contrary, the Catholic Church virtually invented the scientific method! The Church has sponsored and blessed scientific research, and the Church embraces many scientific theories. Many Catholic priests actually have college degrees in science! In fact, the modern "big bang" theory, on the origin of the universe, was invented by a Catholic priest,[14] who was in good standing with the Church. What the Catholic Church does *not* do is teach science as if it were religious doctrine, and insists

---

13 *Usus Antiquior* or the Extraordinary Form of the Roman Rite

14 Father Georges Lemaître (1894 - 1966)

26

that science, like all human disciplines, must be subject to a moral code.[15] Catholics are free to believe in evolution as well, if they so choose, so long as they understand that it was God who created man in his image, and that humans are not a product of random chance. The idea being that whatever scientific processes God used to create the universe and man are open for debate. What is not open for debate is the religious truth that God created all things and that man was created in God's image.

QUESTION: Why is Catholic worship so organised and structured compared to most Protestant worship?

ANSWER: Catholic worship is based in liturgy, and this liturgy comes primarily from ancient Jewish worship, both in the Temple and synagogues, and from the Biblical revelation that God is worshipped in heaven through liturgy.[16] The word "liturgy" is a Biblical word (Luke 1:23; Acts 13:2; Romans 15:16; 2nd Corinthians 9:12; Philippians 2:14-17, 25, 30; Hebrews 8:2 & 6) and comes from a Greek composite word *leitourgia* (λειτουργία) meaning "the duty [or work] of the people." This is the prescribed method of public worship God gave to the Hebrew people in their Temple rites which was carried over into the synagogues. The celebrant recites a passage of Scripture, and the people respond with Scripture, or else a response based on Scripture.

The idea is to present an organised and dignified way through which people can express their personal relationship with God publicly and in community, for God has made his new covenant in Christ with his Church not the individual (Matthew 26:28; Luke 1:72; Romans 11:27; Hebrews 8:8; Hebrews 8:10; Hebrews 10:16). Individuals share in that covenant by becoming part of the larger community (Church) with which that covenant was made. The liturgy is merely a public expression of this. The

---

15 Catechism of the Catholic Church; paragraph 2293

16 Images of heavenly worship from the Book of Revelation

Catholic Church has many liturgical rituals, but the two main rituals are the Divine Liturgy (often called the "Holy Mass") in which Holy Communion is celebrated, and the Divine Office (also called the "Liturgy of the Hours").

The Divine Office is the official prayer liturgy of the Catholic Church and it is required daily reading for clergy. Laymen may optionally participate in it too. This Divine Office comes to us directly from the Temple prayer liturgy in ancient Israel, and is based heavily on the Psalms of David. Prayers are set aside for certain times of the day, and the Bible tells us about the apostles going up to the Temple to pray this liturgy at certain times of the day (Acts 3:1).

The Divine Liturgy (Holy Mass) is the official celebration of the Church, and it is obligatory for all Catholics on every Sunday and certain holy days during the year. This Divine Liturgy (Holy Mass) is a composite of two Jewish liturgies. The first half is the Liturgy of the Word, which comes to Catholicism directly from the Jewish synagogue liturgy. The second half is the Liturgy of the Eucharist, and this comes to us from the Jewish Passover seder combined with prayers used by Jewish priests in the ancient Temple period. Together, the Liturgy of the Word leads us into the Liturgy of the Eucharist. The whole thing marks a continuity between the Church and ancient Israel.

In contrast, when Protestants broke with the Catholic Church in the sixteenth century, they modified their liturgy accordingly. Anglicans and Lutherans initially made very little modifications. In contrast, Reformed and Anabaptists made rather large changes. As we go down through history we reach the modern Baptist, Pentecostal and Evangelical churches. They have stripped away a great deal of liturgy from their weekly services. However, they still retain a shell of liturgy. For example; certain times are designated for singing, other times for praying, and still another time for instruction. At various points during this liturgical shell, the congregation will stand up or sit down. While this is obviously less regimented and structured than Catholic liturgy, it is a shell of liturgy nonetheless.

QUESTION: Why is the Catholic Church so rich when so many of its members are poor?

ANSWER: That depends on what you mean by "rich." The accusation is levelled by some that the Catholic Church hordes money while it lets its members starve, and that such dire poverty is not seen among most Protestant churches. First and foremost, let's get a few things straight. The Catholic Church is not "rich." It is the largest charitable organisation in the world; feeding, sheltering and clothing more people than any other. It is also the largest provider of free educational and medical services on the planet. If you want to say the Catholic Church is "rich" in that it has a lot of resources to draw upon, that is one thing, but to say it hordes its money while letting its members languish in poverty is completely and totally false.

Priests and bishops usually take vows of poverty, which means they get paid a very meagre salary, and usually own very few possessions. They also usually live in very humble apartments or share houses with other clergy. As for the instruments and edifices of Catholic worship; such as beautiful altars, vestments, silverware, shrines and massive basilicas, we must remember that these were donated by the people, specifically for the purpose of worship. This is because, in spite of their economic state in life, they *want to* worship God in a dignified way fitting for the Divine King Jesus. Thus these things are dedicated to God alone. This is absolutely Biblical when we consider the Old Testament descriptions of Temple worship during ancient times.

It's more than that however, unlike many Protestant churches, which are based primarily in the rich industrialised world, the Catholic Church is truly a universal Church, which is primarily based in the developing third-world. Thus the Catholic Church is truly a Church of the poor. That being said she champions the rights of the poor, which consist of many things, but one of those rights is the right to worship God in the same way the rich would, showing no distinction or partiality between rich and poor. We see this same advocation for the poor in the Temple worship of the Jews during ancient times (Leviticus 5:11). The rich would bring their lambs and oxen for sacrifice, while the poor brought their pigeons and turtle-doves, or just "flour" in cases of extreme poverty, but the priest would show no partiality between them. Everyone offered their sacrifices equally in the same glorious Temple of marble and gold, which was dedicated exclusively to God for use by everyone. A similar mentality holds true in the Catholic Church. The poor may be poor, but that does not prohibit them from being brought into the palace of King Jesus – a Catholic parish or basilica. It is after all, just as much for them as for the rich and middle class.

It is a common assumption, and a false one, that the Catholic Church hordes money because of the beautiful instruments and edifices of Catholic worship. Such assumptions only illustrate a lack of understanding of what these things are for, and a lack of understanding of how the Catholic Church uses the overwhelming vast majority of its resources to help the poor.

CHAPTER THREE
SPECIFIC QUESTIONS

QUESTION: Why do Catholics call priests "father" when the Bible says "call no man father?"

ANSWER: The passage that some use to support the idea that Catholics shouldn't call a priest "father" is found in Matthew 23:9 wherein Jesus commanded his followers to call no man "teacher" or "father." This passage is commonly cited against the Catholic practise of calling priests "father." However, when we look at this passage in context we see that Jesus is not prohibiting the use of the word "father" but rather rebuking the religious leaders who do not serve their people. He is rebuking the Pharisees of his time because they are called "rabbi" (which literally means "teacher" or "great one") and accept the religious honour and prestige without embracing the sacrifice and humility that is supposed to go along with it. Jesus is commanding his disciples (later apostles) not to be like that. He doesn't want them to think they are greater than the people they are shepherding. He wants them to think of themselves as servants of the people.

Clearly the titles of "rabbi" and "father" are not prohibited in and of themselves. Jesus accepted the title of "rabbi" on many occasions. Jesus called Abraham "father" (Matthew 3:9). Saint Stephen called the Jewish leaders "fathers" (Acts 7:2) just before he was martyred by them. Are we to believe that Saint Stephen disobeyed Jesus by calling men "father" just before he was martyred? Saint Paul also called the Jewish leaders "fathers" (Acts 21:40; Acts 22:1). Are we to believe Saint Paul was disobeying Jesus Christ by doing this? Saint Paul also refers to Saint Timothy as his *"beloved son in faith"* – (1st Timothy 1:2) If Timothy is a "son" in the faith, then what do we suppose Timothy called Saint Paul in the faith? Saint Paul specifically told the Corinthian Christians that he was their "spiritual father" (1st Corinthians 4:14-15). He said the same to his disciple Philemon (Philemon 10).

When we read the writings of the early Christians of the first few centuries, it becomes clear that the practise of referring to Christian leaders as "father" was commonplace. This is because the early Christians understood Jesus prohibition on the use of the title "father" in its appropriate context. Jesus was addressing arrogance in leadership. He was not prohibiting the use of certain titles. We Catholics call our priests "father" because that's how we look at them. We see them as paternal guardians of our parish family. They serve the role of a "father" in this spiritual setting. In Catholic Christianity, we look at the Church as one big family. We address priests as "fathers," nuns as "sisters" and monks as "brothers." We don't do this because *we* think they are somehow superior, nor do *they* think they are superior. Rather, we do it simply as a sign of family affection.

QUESTION: Why do Catholics confess their sins to a priest when they could go directly to God?

ANSWER: We confess our sins to a priest because Jesus told us to. You see, while Jesus was on earth he regularly forgave people's sins. The religious leaders of his time were indignant about this, asking: "*Who can forgive sins, but God only?*" – (Mark 2:7) So Jesus received some really harsh judgement from the religious leaders of his time over this. However, he proved to them that he did have the authority to forgive sins by doing miracles that only God could do. No Christian today denies that Jesus has the authority to forgive sins (Matthew 9:2-8). That is beyond dispute now. Catholics however, take the whole testimony of Scripture into account.

Not only did Jesus have the authority to forgive sins, but he also shared this authority with his apostles and their successors: "*He *said therefore to them again: Peace be to you. As the Father hath sent me, I also send you. When he had said this, he breathed on them; and he said to them: Receive ye the Holy Ghost. Whose sins you shall forgive, they are forgiven them; and whose sins you shall retain, they are retained."* – (John 20:21-23) This one passage alone demonstrates beyond the shadow of a doubt that Jesus shared his authority to forgive (and retain) sins with his apostles. The apostles then hand-picked their own successors (Acts 1:20-26) and likewise transferred this ministry to them (2nd Corinthians 5:17-20).

For Catholics, this is simply a matter of believing the Bible and taking what it says seriously. Either Jesus gave some men his authority to forgive sins, or he did not, and the Bible clearly says he did. Now when we Catholics commit a sin, we do confess those sins directly to God, both before confession and during confession. The priest then, by the authority he has based on Jesus' own words, dispenses Christ's forgiveness in an official way, as if Jesus Christ himself had said it. The real question here is not why do Catholics go to a priest? But rather, why do other Christians *not* go to a priest when the Bible specifically says that Jesus gave some men the authority to forgive sins in his place? Since the earliest days of the Church, Christians have always approached their church leaders for absolution. What makes some Christians today think they're so different? Catholics don't see any difference at all. The early Christians approached their leaders for reconciliation and so do we.

QUESTION: Why can't Catholic priests be married?

ANSWER: Shh. Don't tell anyone, but actually they can be married. That's a big secret you see. With papal permission, any Catholic priest can give up the priesthood to have a wife and family,[17] and since all of them are fairly well educated with college degrees, they'll have no problem picking up a good secular job or

---

17 Code of Canon Law: 291

starting a family business. Nuns and monks are the same way. They can, at any time, choose to leave their orders to pursue a secular life in holy matrimony. Most of them are highly educated too. Nobody is a "prisoner" of his or her religious vocation.

There is another secret. It is possible for a Catholic priest to be both a priest and married at the same time. In fact, there are hundreds of married Catholic priests throughout North America and Europe. You see, the required vow of clerical celibacy is a discipline not a doctrine, and it only applies to the Roman Rite of the Catholic Church. There are twenty-three rites that make up the Catholic Church. A "rite" is a particular way of being Catholic. Each rite has its own liturgy, traditions and disciplines, but all of them are part of the Catholic Church and are in full communion with the pope in Rome. The Roman Rite is just one of these twenty-three rites, but it is the largest, and it is the most well known. Married men are permitted to become Catholic priests in twenty-two of these twenty-three rites.[18] In spite of that, however, many of these men choose celibacy instead. We don't see much of these other rites in the Western world except in big cities. In the Eastern world however, they are quite common.

Only the Roman Rite strictly ordains celibate men to the priesthood, and even then, there are exceptions to this rule. For example; if married Protestant ministers wish to convert to Catholicism and become Catholic priests, the Roman Rite has been known to allow them to do this on a case-by-case basis.[19] There is also the Anglican Ordinariate of the Roman Rite, which permits this exception on a much larger scale.[20]

The discipline of clerical celibacy strictly within the Roman Rite was instituted during the latter Middle Ages for very practical reasons. It can be changed at any time. That being said, as of the

---

18 Catechism of the Catholic Church; paragraph 1580

19 *Sacerdotalis coelibatus*, n. 42

20 *Anglicanorum coetibus*, VI. §1, §2

date of this writing, there is no indication that anyone plans to change it anytime soon. A celibate priesthood has worked well for the Roman Rite, ensuring its rapid growth around the world.

The idea of clerical celibacy is Biblical. Jesus was celibate and he praised those who chose a celibate life to serve the Kingdom of God (Matthew 19:12). Saint Paul, who was also celibate, actually recommended celibacy for anyone working in full-time ministry (1st Corinthians 7:32-35). The vow of celibacy among women in the Church (early nuns) was even commonplace in the Apostolic era while Saint Paul was still writing the New Testament (1st Timothy 5:9-12).

In response to the recent growing interest of married Catholic men wanting to enter ministry, the Roman Rite of the Catholic Church has also reopened the position of the permanent diaconate for married Catholic men who feel such a calling. The diaconate allows married Roman Catholic men to become deacons in the Catholic Church.[21] They assist in the liturgies of the Church, they can preach homilies (sermons), teach the faith, minister to the sick, baptise the faithful and perform weddings. Basically a Catholic deacon can do just about anything a Protestant minister does. The only thing a Catholic deacon does not do is celebrate the Eucharist, hear confessions and anoint the sick, but then a Protestant minister cannot do these things either. At least, he can't from a Catholic perspective anyway. In many ways a Catholic deacon is parallel to a Protestant minister (or "pastor") in function and responsibility. The diaconate serves as an excellent way for married Catholic men to participate in the vocation of Church ministry in an official way. That is, if they are called to it of course.

QUESTION: Why do Catholics use the rosary when the Bible says not to pray in "vain repetitions?"

---

21 Code of Canon Law: 1031 §2

ANSWER: First of all, Catholics are not required to pray the rosary. It is considered a "private devotion," but it is nevertheless an extremely popular one among Catholics (even among some Anglicans), and since the Middle Ages has been used as a substitute of the Divine Office (Liturgy of the Hours) among lay Christians. Many stories of healing, conversion and answered prayer are attributed to regular recitation of the holy rosary.

The one and only Scripture passage often used to support the idea that God forbids repetitious prayer is in Matthew 6:7 and comes specifically from some older English translations of the Bible. *"But when ye pray, use not vain repetitions, as the heathen do: for they think that they shall be heard for their much speaking."* – (Matthew 6:7)[22] Very few English translations use the phrase "vain repetitions." Most instead translate it as "babbling" or "babbling on," and this is probably a reference to the events recorded in 1st Kings 18:25-29 when the Pagan priests of Baal called upon their idol for hours while cutting themselves.

The problem here appears to be the Greek word *battalogeo* (βατταλογέω) which some older English versions translate as "vain repetitions." The word itself is a contraction of two Greek words: *batta* and *logeo*. Literally translated, *batta* means "babbling" and *logeo* means "words" or "many words." So transliterated the phrase in question reads: "use not babbling words." For some unknown reason, the older English translators decided to put more emphasis on the plurality of "words" in *logeo*, and less emphasis on "babbling" in *batta*. Thus instead of translating *battalogeo* as "babbling words" or "babbling on and on" they came up with "vain repetitions." Go figure! Needless to say, this is no longer the case with most English translations. The problem seems to have begun with the Geneva Bible (1599 AD), which was outspokenly anti-Catholic. The King James Version then followed suit and the rest is history. Regardless

---

22 King James Version, 1611 AD

of the political rationale behind it, this way of translating the verse is just plain wrong.

Jesus did not give a blanket condemnation of repeating a meaningful prayer to the true God in Matthew 6:7. On the contrary, the original Greek tells us that what he forbade was the senseless babbling that some people once did in a vain attempt to get their idol's attention. As in all things we should look to the example of Jesus to understand his intent. Jesus himself repeated his prayer to God the Father in Matthew 26:44, and he praised the tax collector who repeated his prayer multiple times in Luke 18:13. Saint Paul told the Thessalonians to pray without ceasing (1st Thessalonians 5:17) and the Book of Revelation tells us that God is surrounded by creatures who pray the same thing over and over again (Revelation 4:8). There is nothing in the Bible that forbids repetitive meaningful prayers. In fact, the Bible actually published them (Psalm 136). What is forbidden is senseless babbling that doesn't make sense, so as to try to get God's attention, as if he somehow has difficulty hearing us.

QUESTION: Is the pope the Antichrist?

ANSWER: While this question may seem ridiculous to many people, you might be surprised to discover just how many Protestants actually believe it, or are at least suspicious of it. The notion comes from the first Protestant reformer himself – Martin Luther[23] – in the sixteenth century, who asserted that the *office* of the papacy is the Antichrist. That's not to say any particular pope, but the office of the papacy itself.[24] So when German Protestants began

---

23 Martin Luther – the sixteenth century German Protestant reformer, not to be confused with Martin Luther King, the twentieth century American civil rights activist.

24 While most Lutherans today have dropped this teaching, some have not. In particular, as of the date of this writing, the Missouri Synod Lutheran Church (LCMS), as well as the Wisconsin Synod Lutheran Church (WELS), still officially teach that the "office" of the papacy (not the pope himself) is the Antichrist.

to mix with English Protestants in the United States during the nineteenth century, you can imagine what an explosive combination this created. As new American-style Protestant denominations were formed, the office of the papacy went from being the Antichrist on a purely philosophical level, to the actual incarnation of evil itself!

This notion has become very popular among some Baptist, Evangelical and Pentecostal groups in the United States, and is a bit humorous when you really stop and think about it. Before we start levelling the accusation of "Antichrist" at anybody, or any office, it might help to actually understand what the Bible has to say about it. After all, the whole idea of "Antichrist" is a Biblical concept.

So what does the Bible say about the Antichrist? Well, for starters, the Bible tells us that the "spirit of antichrist" was alive and well even during the Apostolic age (1st John 2:18). It also tells us that in order to be antichrist in any way, one must deny that Jesus of Nazareth is the promised Jewish Messiah (1st John 2:22). One must also deny that God the Son came to earth in the form of flesh and blood (1st John 4:3; 2nd John 1:7). These are the only four times the word "antichrist" appears in the Scriptures. So based on the Biblical definition, to be an antichrist (or even THE Antichrist) one must deny that Jesus of Nazareth is the promised Messiah *and* one must deny that God the Son came to earth in the form of human flesh. Sorry, that's just the Biblical definition, and since the term "Antichrist" is a Biblical term, just like the term "Christ" itself, it has no real meaning outside this Biblical definition.

Now since every pope since the time of St. Peter has affirmed that Jesus of Nazareth is the Messianic Son of God, that sort of disqualifies every pope in history from being an antichrist. Of course, the office of the papacy itself was literally _founded_ on Saint Peter's affirmation that Jesus of Nazareth is the promised Messianic Son of God (Matthew 16:15-19), so that disqualifies the papal office from being antichrist. Since the pope literally teaches, and his office is literally founded upon, the belief that Jesus of Nazareth is the Messianic Son of God, it is literally impossible (in every Biblical sense) for the pope, or his papal office, to be the Antichrist in any way. Again, sorry, but the Bible speaks for itself here. To assert that the pope or the papacy is somehow, in any way, the Antichrist, is to completely deny the plain and clear teaching of the Bible on this matter. Now, if some people want to go ahead and call the pope the Antichrist anyway, then they can go ahead, but in doing so, the rest of us need to understand they are directly contradicting the Bible when they do this.

QUESTION: Doesn't God hate religion and isn't Christianity really about having a personal relationship with God?

ANSWER: If God hates religion he certainly has a funny way of showing it, since he actually invented the most complex and demanding religion in the world – ancient Judaism. It has become in vogue in recent decades for some Evangelical Protestants to insist that God is opposed to religion in general, and prefers people to instead have a personal relationship with him. While it is certainly true that God wants us to have a personal relationship with him, and that popes have spoken extensively on this very thing,[25] it is also true that God never intended such a personal relationship to be private.

There is a difference you see, between personal and private, as this personal relationship we are supposed to have with God is simultaneously supposed to be a public one. God made his new covenant with a community not individuals. Individuals can share in that covenant by being initiated into the community God has covenanted with. Religion is simply the way people organise their personal relationship with God into a public and communal

---

25 Pope John Paul II, speech to bishops of Southern Germany, December 4, 1992; Pope Benedict XVI, Angelus, Vatican City, February 26, 2012

expression that is both orderly and dignified.[26] Thus religion and relationship complement each other. They are not opposed to one another.

In the case of Christianity, that religion was organised by the apostles of Jesus Christ and their successors (the popes and bishops). There is nothing in the Scriptures that condemns religion in and of itself. However, there are plenty of Scripture passages that condemn the hypocritical abuse of religion for personal gain. So no, God does not hate religion, and yes, Christianity is about having a personal relationship with Jesus Christ. That personal relationship is public, not private, and Christian religion helps us express it publicly and in community.

---

26 Catechism of the Catholic Church; paragraphs 1140 & 2105

CHAPTER FOUR
THE BIBLE

QUESTION: Do Catholics believe in the Bible?

ANSWER: Yes! In fact, Catholics invented the Bible. Shocking as that may sound it is historically accurate to say that. The New Testament did not exist as a single compilation prior to 367 AD. Before then most of the writings of the New Testament were on parchment scrolls and scattered throughout the churches of Europe, Asia and Northern Africa. They were mixed together with other writings that were orthodox but not necessarily inspired Scripture. No two areas had the exact same scrolls, nor the exact same *number* of scrolls. It was all rather chaotic. So in response to the Arian heresy in the fourth century, the Catholic Church commissioned its bishops to find out which scrolls should belong to a universal New Testament that everyone would use. Many committees were held to determine this based on Catholic Tradition, when in 367 AD a Catholic bishop in Northern Africa, named Athanasius, commissioned a particular set of twenty-seven scrolls consisting of the writings of Matthew through Revelation. Three Catholic synods were then held to ratify this list, and in 405 AD Pope Innocent declared these twenty-seven scrolls to be the universal New Testament for all Christians! This is the same New Testament we use today, even in Protestant churches, thanks to the hard and faithful work of the Catholic Church sixteen hundred years ago.[27]

QUESTION: Do Catholics read the Bible?

ANSWER: Yes, we actually do, perhaps even more so than most Protestants. That's because some of us not only read the Bible

---

27 Catechism of the Catholic Church; paragraph 120

on our own, but we have the Bible read to us at mass every day of the week. In fact, if a Catholic simply attends mass every Sunday, he will have heard nearly the entire Bible read to him over the course of three years. If he attends mass every day, which a small few do, he will have heard nearly the whole Bible read to him three times in four years. This doesn't even include the liturgy itself, which is chalk full of Scripture passages from the Bible. Just attending mass is like going to a Bible-fest! The priest reads the Bible. The people respond with memorised responses heavily based on Biblical passages. Of course, if the Catholic then prays the Divine Office (Liturgy of the Hours) he again is exposed to an extremely hefty portion of Scripture. Some Catholics attend Bible studies on top of that, and some read and study the Bible on their own. In fact, the Catholic Church actively exhorts Catholics to read and study the Bible.[28] What Catholics do not generally do is memorise Biblical passages in rote with their chapter and verse numbers attached. This is a common Protestant practise not often shared by Catholics. So if one is expecting to hear a Catholic rattle off a Biblical passage with a chapter and verse attached, one will likely be disappointed, and because of that, it might superficially appear that the Catholic is Biblically illiterate, though this is actually not the case at all. Now if a Catholic doesn't attend mass, then he's not a good Catholic, and of course by not attending mass, he's probably not reading or hearing much of the Bible either. The same is true of Protestants who don't attend church.

QUESTION: Why do Catholic Bibles have more books than Protestant Bibles?

ANSWER: The short answer is to say that Catholics kept the books that Protestants removed from the Bible. Now here is the long answer.

---

28 Catechism of the Catholic Church; paragraphs 104, 131 & 133

42

You see, the canon of the Bible was basically settled in 405 AD. However, over a thousand years later, the German Reformer Martin Luther decided to move seven books from the Old Testament (Tobit, Judith, 1st Maccabees, 2nd Maccabees, Wisdom, Sirach and Baruch) into a separate section he called *apocrypha* (meaning "disputed"). Luther then moved portions of the Old Testament books of Esther and Daniel into this *apocrypha* section as well. Now in Luther's defense we could say that he was only following the standardised Jewish canon being used in Europe at that time. However, what many people don't know is that the standardised scriptural canon, used in mediaeval Jewish synagogues, developed as the result of mainstream Judaism coming under the control of the Pharisee party after the fall of the Jerusalem Temple in 70 AD. The Pharisees had their own list of canonical books, which was shorter than the Old Testament canonical books used by the apostles, and throughout most of the Jewish communities in the Mediterranean world.

The apostles, on the other hand, primarily used the Greek translation of the Jewish canon (*Septuagint*) which contained more books than the Pharisaical Jewish canon (*Tanakh*). This Greek Jewish Bible (*Septuagint*) was the canon of Scripture used by the majority of Jews outside of Palestine in the first century. So this is the one the apostles preferred and quoted from frequently in their own writings (gospels and epistles). As the good news of Jesus Christ spread throughout the ancient world, Jews came under tremendous pressure to choose between the Christians and the Pharisees. Those Jews who sided with the Christians just became known as "Christians" along with the rest, and were eventually "put out of the synagogue" (excommunicated from Judaism). Those Jews who sided with the Pharisees then adopted many Pharisaical practices, which included: the rejection of Christian claims of Jesus as the promised Messiah, the use of the shorter Pharisaical canon (*Tanakh*), the mandatory reading of that canon in Hebrew (as opposed to Greek), and a host of other standardisations. Thus the standardised Jewish canon throughout the Mediterranean world came to be shorter than the Christian Old Testament canon (*Septuagint*).[29] So the real question in play here is this. Who has the authority to determine the Christian Old Testament canon? Does that authority belong to the apostles and early Church? Or does it belong to the late first-century Pharisee party that rejected Christian claims? Luther may have had his own reasons for moving some Old Testament books out of the official canon and into his "apocrypha" section, but the premise of this decision is identical to that of the late first-century Pharisees. He based it on an authority that was non-apostolic. Today, Protestant scholars go to great lengths to explain why some of these books should be excluded from the Christian Old Testament canon, but again, they base this on academics, not actual apostolic authority. The fact is, the apostles primarily used, and quoted from, the *Septuagint*. The early Church regarded this as equally authoritative and on par with the Hebrew *Tanakh* used by the Pharisees. If the longer Old Testament *Septuagint* was good enough for the apostles and early Church, why should it not be good enough for us today?

Martin Luther then tried to remove four books from the New Testament as well (Hebrews, James, Jude and Revelation). His rationale was that these books didn't carry the same weight as the rest based on his academic studies. In other words, they didn't agree with his theology.

His removal of the Old Testament books from the regular canon, along with his shortening of Esther and Daniel, became a very popular trend among Protestants throughout Europe.[30]

---

29 Except in Ethiopia. Ethiopian Jews did not come under the influence of the Pharisees after the fall of the Temple in AD 70. So they still use the Greek translated *Septuagint*.

30 Thirty-Nine Articles of Religion (Anglicanism 1563 AD); Westminster Confession of Faith (Calvinism 1647 AD); from these two confessions come the sixty-six book Protestant canon of the Bible.

However, his attempted removal of the four New Testament books was ultimately rejected by all, and eventually forgotten to history.

The Catholic Church however, does not believe that any modern scholar, priest or bishop, (not even the pope himself) has the authority to alter the Biblical text regardless of the level of academic reasoning that goes behind it.[31] So Catholics use the longer Old Testament canon originally used by the apostles and early Christians.

It is interesting to note that most Protestant Bibles continued to print the so-called *apocrypha* books up until the 1880s. Even the original version of the highly esteemed King James Bible retained the so-called *apocrypha* books, and continued to print them until this time. The complete absence of the so-called *apocryphal* books from virtually all Protestant Bibles is a relatively modern phenomenon unique to the twentieth century. In recent decades, however, it has become in vogue for some Protestant Bible publishers to print Bibles that include all of the books they previously removed. So, just a century after completely removing those books from their printed Bibles, some Protestant publishers are starting to put them back in. Is your Christian Bible complete? Or are you using an older truncated version? See above to check if it contains the "missing" Old Testament books.

QUESTION: Do Catholics follow the Bible alone?

ANSWER: No. Catholics do not follow the Bible **alone** because it's not Biblical to do that. The idea of following the Bible alone comes from the German reformer Martin Luther, who in 1520 AD declared "*Sola Scriptura*" as one of his five "solas" or pillars of German Protestantism. The Latin phrase "Sola Scriptura"

---

31 *De Canonicis Scripturis*, Council of Trent (1546 AD); Session 11, Council of Florence (1442 AD); Synod of Rome (382 AD); Synod of Hippo (393 AD); Synod of Carthage (397 AD); Decree of Pope Innocent I (405 AD)

means "Scripture Only" or the "Bible Alone." There is no Biblical passage that can back this idea. In fact, the Bible suggests the exact opposite. The canon of Scripture itself, which is the list of books that make up the Bible, is not anywhere recorded in the actual text of Scripture. So if we go by the concept of the "Bible Alone," we don't really know what books should belong in the Bible to begin with.

The Bible also tells us specifically to follow the traditions of the Church (1st Corinthians 11:1), whether written in the Scriptures, or given orally (2nd Thessalonians 2:15). It tells us to shun those who do not keep the traditions of the Church (2nd Thessalonians 3:6) and tells us that Scripture should not even be interpreted independently of the Church (2nd Peter 1:20 & 2nd Peter 3:15-16). Jesus himself commanded his own apostles to follow the traditions of the Jewish leaders (Matthew 23:2-3) because they held an authority of succession from Moses. What Jesus condemned was not tradition in and of itself, but rather the hypocrisy of the Jewish leaders of his time, who abused tradition for their own financial and political gain (Matthew 15:1-8).

No, Catholics do not follow the Bible alone, because the Bible basically tells us not to. Catholics instead follow both sacred Scripture (the Bible) and sacred Tradition, which is conveyed to us through the teaching authority of the Catholic Church.

QUESTION: Wait! Doesn't the Bible tell us to follow the Bible alone?

ANSWER: No, it does not. As I said above, there is not a single Biblical passage that instructs Christians to follow the Bible **alone**. That being the case, no Christian can be held to Martin Luther's rule of *Sola Scriptura*. Perhaps some Christians may voluntarily submit to it, but no Christian can be forced to follow it.

One common objection used by some Protestants is found in the second epistle of Saint Paul to Timothy: *"All scripture, inspired of God, is profitable to teach, to reprove, to correct, to instruct in justice, That the man of God may be perfect, furnished to every good work."* – (2nd Timothy 3:16-17) However, it should be pointed out here that the passage specifically says "<u>All</u> Scripture" not "<u>Only</u> Scripture." So it can in no way be used as a prooftext for *Sola Scriptura*. Another common objection is found in Saint Paul's first epistle to the Church in Corinth: *"I have applied all this to myself and Apollos for your benefit, brethren, that you may learn by us <u>not to go beyond what is written</u>, that none of you may be puffed up in favor of one against another."* – (1st Corinthians 4:6)[32] This is how the passage is commonly translated into most modern English versions of the Bible, and because of this, it is commonly used as a prooftext for *Sola Scriptura* by a whole lot of Protestants. However, this is one example where I think the older English versions do a much better job picking up on the nuance of Jewish idioms. Here we have the same verse from the 1899 Douay-Rheims version: *"But these things, brethren, I have in a figure transferred to myself and to Apollo, for your sakes; that in us you may learn, that one be <u>not puffed up against the other for another, above that which is written</u>."* – (1st Corinthians 4:6) Then of course the much esteemed 1611 King James Bible so eloquently puts the same verse this way: *"And these things, brethren, I have in a figure transferred to myself and to Apollos for your sakes; that ye might learn in us <u>not to think of men above that which is written</u>, that no one of you be puffed up for one against another."* — (1st Corinthians 4:6)[33] As you can see, once the nuance of this Jewish idiom is translated it radically clarifies the inferred meaning of the passage. It's also contextual, you see, because in this chapter, Saint Paul is telling the Corinthians not to be divided in their leadership. Nowhere in this chapter does Saint Paul discuss the canon of

---

32 Revised Standard Version – Catholic Edition (emphasis mine)

33 King James Version (emphasis mine)

Scripture, or why Christians should only believe in the Scriptures alone.

Then of course, there is the all too common objection from the Book of Revelation that pronounces a curse upon anyone who adds to the Scriptures (Revelation 22:18). However, this is a curse upon anyone who adds to the Book of Revelation in particular, and it is followed by a curse upon anyone who removes portions of the book as well (Revelation 22:19). It pertains specifically to the Book of Revelation and has nothing to do with extra-Biblical traditions. To say that it does is to do gross violence to the context of the passage.

There is nothing in the Bible that limits Christian belief or practice to the Bible alone. In all fairness to Martin Luther, what is now commonly understood as *Sola Scriptura* in most Protestant communities is not what he actually meant when he coined the phrase. The original definition of *Sola Scriptura*, from a Lutheran perspective, is that Scripture is the <u>only infallible</u> source of divine revelation. Therefore, all other things, including Christian traditions and leadership, must be subject to the infallible teaching of Scripture alone. From a Catholic perspective, there are problems with this understanding. As the canon of Scripture itself was created by the infallible proclamations of the Church. Therefore, logic would dictate that sources of infallibility can likewise be found outside of the Bible, both in Apostolic Tradition and the occasional proclamations of the Church. Again, the Bible points to the Church (not itself) as the pillar and foundation of truth (1st Timothy 3:15). This however, is an argument for Catholic and Lutheran theologians to hammer out in the course of ecumenical discussions. What *Sola Scriptura* has effectively become however, in the emerging Protestant mainstream, might even be considered heretical from a Lutheran point of view. Namely the notion that if a doctrine is not directly (or implicitly) found in the Bible; it is not to be believed. As far as I know, this was never Luther's intent when he coined the term. Unfortunately, this very anti-Biblical notion is becoming more and more popular in the emerging Protestant mainstream. It is both unreasonable, and unbiblical, for Protestants to insist that every article of faith and practice be found in the Bible. It's also self-contradicting. Protestants would do well to go back to Martin Luther's original intent for *Sola Scriptura* and acknowledge at least the possibility of legitimate extra-Biblical beliefs and practices. Then we can reasonably discuss the authority for such things. To just dismiss them however, out of hand, simply because they are not directly found in the Bible, is a very unbiblical thing to do.

QUESTION: Didn't the medieval Catholic Church chain Bibles to altars, burn vernacular Bible translations and intentionally try to prevent the people from reading the Scriptures by keeping them in Latin?

ANSWER: The Catholic Church has *never* tried to keep the Scriptures away from the people. In fact, the Catholic Church was the first to commission vernacular translations of the Bible. The Latin Bible itself was a vernacular translation from the original Greek and Hebrew text. As for vernacular translations into modern languages, many within the Catholic Church actually worked very hard to make this happen. Let's take the English language for example. In the late seventh century, a large compilation of the Bible was translated into Old English by Saint Bede. Some time later, Richard Rolle made a significant update as the English language changed, translating the Biblical Psalter into Middle English in the early fourteenth century. All of these were done by Catholics for Catholic England long before the English Reformation. To say the Catholic Church was negligent in translating the Scriptures into modern vernaculars is patently untrue. The only times in history when the Church permitted Bibles to be burned were when it was determined that the particular translation in question was flawed and presented heresy. In such cases, properly translated Bibles were offered to replace them.

As for chaining Bibles to altars, that did happen a very long time ago, but not to keep the Bible away from the people. On the contrary, it was to make sure Bibles were *not* taken away from the people. You see, back during the Middle Ages, before the age of the printing press, Bibles were copied by hand. Thus they were extremely expensive. One Bible could easily cost an entire year's salary of the average working man. The problem was that with such an expensive book sitting on the altar, it would be very easy for it to be stolen, taken to another city, and sold at a very handsome profit. So to prevent this from happening, and to make sure the people of the parish retained access to the sacred Scriptures, these expensive Bibles were chained to the altars for safe keeping. This way, any common parishioner (assuming he was literate) could easily go to the church on any day, walk up to the altar, and always have a Bible available to read to his heart's content.

Now, the false assertion that the Catholic Church was trying to keep the Scriptures away from the people in the Middle Ages is often made with the false assumption that the Catholic Church was trying to hide the gospel from the people. This again is patently false, and a bit ridiculous when you stop and think about it. The whole mission of the Catholic Church has always been to convey the message of the gospel, and in the vastly illiterate world of the Middle Ages, she did this by using all means at her disposal. Of course, clergy were trained to read the Scriptures, and convey them to the people in their regular homilies (sermons). Likewise poems and songs, which could be easily memorised, were employed for this purpose too. In addition, the Church hired artists to paint and carve images, which could likewise be used as teaching tools to educate the populace. We use this exact same pictorial method in illustrated children's books today. The Catholic Church did a remarkable job conveying the gospel to a world without literacy, the printing press, television, email or the Internet.

CHAPTER FIVE
MARY AND THE SAINTS

QUESTION: Do Catholics worship Mary?

ANSWER: No, Catholics do not worship[34] Mary, nor do we worship anyone or anything other than the Trinitarian God: Father, Son and Holy Spirit. The Catholic Church condemns the worship of anyone or anything else as idolatry[35] and such idolatry could be punishable by excommunication, if such an idolator does not repent.

QUESTION: If Catholics do not worship Mary, why then do Catholics pray to Mary?

ANSWER: Catholics pray to Mary, other Saints and the holy angels, because we do not believe prayer, in and of itself, is worship. Catholics understand worship in the Biblical sense, which usually involves the presentation of an actual flesh and blood sacrifice (Genesis 4:4; Genesis 8:20; Exodus 22:20; 1st Samuel 15:22; Romans 5:10; 1st Corinthians 5:7; 1st Peter 2:5). This, coupled with the act of adoration (full submission of the mind, body, soul and will) is how Catholics understand worship in the usual Biblical sense. In the act of Holy Communion we unite ourselves with Christ's perfect sacrifice thus participating in real Biblical worship.[36] The mere act of prayer is simply to offer requests and does not, in and of itself, constitute worship in the full Biblical sense.

---

34 Worship: meaning *adoration*, to acknowledge as God, and give full act of submission to divinity

35 Catechism of the Catholic Church; paragraphs 2112 - 2114

36 Catechism of the Catholic Church; paragraphs 2099 - 2100

QUESTION: Why pray to Mary and the Saints at all when you can take your prayers directly to God?

ANSWER: As Catholics we do take our prayers directly to God all the time. We do so publicly during the Divine Liturgy (Holy Mass) and also during the Divine Office (Liturgy of the Hours), as well as during the administration of all the sacraments. We also take our prayers directly to God during private devotion and prayers as well. In addition to this, we also pray to Mary, the Saints and the holy angels, because we view them as "prayer partners" in our devotion to God.[37] They assist us in our prayers in the sense that they pray *with* us to God. Just as we ask friends and neighbours in this world to pray for us, so we also ask friends in the next world to pray for us as well. The Bible itself gives us indications that this is a wholesome and acceptable practise (Tobit 12:12; Mark 12:26-27; Mark 9:4; Hebrews 12:1; Revelation 5:8; Revelation 8:4).

QUESTION: How is praying to the Saints not necromancy or witchcraft which is forbidden in the Bible?

ANSWER: There is absolutely nothing in the Bible that forbids praying to the Saints. Jesus himself did it in Mark 9:4.[38] If it's good enough for the Son of God, then it's good enough for us.

The Scripture passage that is commonly used here, in an attempt to equate prayer to Saints with necromancy or witchcraft, is Deuteronomy 18:10 in which God strictly forbids witchcraft. This is then combined with the Scripture that recalls King Saul's encounter with the witch at Endor (1st Samuel 28). Because the witch engaged

---

37 Catechism of the Catholic Church; paragraphs 2683 - 2684

38 While Jesus is divine and able to communicate with the dead freely, he was also a Jewish man under the Law of Moses when he did this. If he broke the Law of Moses he could not be God nor a perfect sacrifice for our sins. Thus simple communication with the dead, through the Holy Spirit, cannot be a violation of God's law.

in conjuring up the dead (a medium), it is mistakenly interpreted that any attempted contact with the dead is a form of witchcraft.

First of all, when Catholics pray to a deceased person, we do not expect that person to answer us in a way we can hear, as is typically expected when one visits a medium. Second, when we pray to a deceased person, we do so through the Holy Spirit, and it is the Holy Spirit who makes that communication possible. We make no attempt to circumvent (get around) God and talk to the dead ourselves, expecting some kind of reply apart from God. That really would be witchcraft and necromancy. The very definition of witchcraft is to attempt to do things apart from God. We Catholics have no desire for this and such things are forbidden by the Church anyway.

As I said, there is no Scriptural prohibition against praying to the Saints and I defy anyone to present me with one. You see, Catholic Christians believe that death is truly conquered in the resurrection of Jesus Christ. We do not believe people in Heaven are really dead. We believe they are living, and they are just as connected to the Holy Spirit as we are, if not more so. They are more finely attuned to what is happening in the Body of Christ than we are. Therefore, we can communicate with them. We can send messages to them, through the Holy Spirit in prayer, and we most certainly can ask them to pray for us, which is what we do. The real question here is to ask; why do some Christians <u>not</u> pray to Saints? Has not the power of death truly been conquered in the resurrection of Jesus Christ? Why do some Christians assert that the dead are truly dead and helpless when the Bible says they are not? (Hebrews 12:1; Revelation 5:8) Perhaps the answer can be found in their refusal to pray to angels as well. They mistake prayer for worship.

QUESTION: Why do Catholics have statues of Mary and other Saints?

ANSWER: Statues, sculptures and paintings of various figures from the Bible, and various persons throughout history, are called icons, and they serve as visual reminders of these persons and the virtues they represent. They are used as visual aids in the same way a Bible serves as a written aid. When one enters a private home it is common to see pictures of family members on the walls, both living and deceased. In the same way, when one enters a Catholic Church, the images of loved ones in the Church are commonplace.[39]

QUESTION: Doesn't the Bible forbid the use of statues and "graven images?"

ANSWER: I certainly hope not, since a photograph of any kind would qualify as a "graven image" even if it is only graven with ink. You better toss those family photos if that is the case! The Biblical passage most commonly used to support the notion that graven images are forbidden by God is Exodus 20:4-5. However, just five chapters later (Exodus 25:18-19) the very same God that supposedly forbade graven images then commanded Moses to make graven images. So which is it? Are we to have graven images or not? Was God effectively saying; "*Make no graven images, except this one?*" Then in Numbers 21:8-9, God again commanded Moses to make a graven image. Then in 1st Kings 6:23-29 and 1st Kings 7:25-45, we see that God actually blessed Solomon's Temple, made in God's honour, which was covered with graven images inside and out! Clearly, God does not have a problem with graven images; not statues, nor icons, nor paintings.

---

39 Catechism of the Catholic Church; paragraphs 1159 - 1162

If we take a closer look at the context of the prohibition against graven images in Exodus 20, we can see that what God was really forbidding was the making of graven images *dedicated to false gods*. What God actually forbade was the worship of false gods, and any image that represented such false divinity. He was not prohibiting the creation and display of graven images in general. Nor did he forbid their use in places of worship dedicated to him. What God forbade was the creation of images that represent a deity (god or goddess) other than himself. For God is not only a jealous God, but he does not contradict himself either. It is illogical to say that God prohibits all graven images, but then commands and blesses the use of graven images. When reading the Bible, remember the Rule of Context, which is "context rules!" To say that God prohibits graven images because of one particular verse, and then just leave it at that, is a gross violation of the rule of context. God does not prohibit graven images! What he prohibits is graven images of false gods. There is a difference.

QUESTION: Why do Catholics believe in the ever virginity of Mary when the Bible talks about the "brothers" of Jesus Christ?

ANSWER: Here is the problem. Jesus spoke Aramaic. The gospel was first proclaimed in Aramaic. In the ancient language of Aramaic, there is no word for cousin, aunt or uncle. These members of extended family are simply referred to as "brothers" and "sisters." The same is true of ancient Hebrew (Genesis 14:12 *compare to* Genesis 14:16).

The references in the New Testament that refer to the "brothers" and "sisters" of Jesus have no Biblical connection to actual blood siblings. In fact, the Scriptures refer to different mothers for some of those named "brothers" of our Lord (Matthew 27:56 *compare to* John 19:25). Of course many refer to a single word *"until"* in Matthew 1:25 to prove that Mary lost her virginity after the birth of Jesus Christ. These same people fail to recognise that the same word *"until"* is used multiple times in Scripture (Matthew 28:20; 1st Corinthians 15:25; 1st Timothy 4:13), and in no way means something changed after a certain event.

Besides the unanimous Tradition of the early Church, what clearly tells us that Jesus had no male siblings, is the fact that as Jesus was dying on the cross, he gave care of his mother to his disciple John rather than to the next male sibling in line as Jewish law would require (John 19:26-27). Are we to believe that Jesus broke Jewish Law immediately before he died? If he did, that would make him a sinner, and thus an imperfect sacrifice. No, Jesus did not (indeed he could not) break the Law of Moses, because as a Jewish man he was under the Law of Moses, and as God he could not sin. So the fact that he gave the care of his mother to somebody who was clearly not his sibling brother indicates that he had no sibling brothers. To say that he did is to make Jesus Christ a sinner while he was on the cross dying for our sins.

QUESTION: Why do Catholics believe Mary was without sin?

ANSWER: Besides the unanimous consensus of the early Church, and plenty of early Christian writings to support that dating back to the second century AD, the greeting of the angel Gabriel is the Biblical reference that clues us in. The angel Gabriel addressed Mary with the Greek word *kecharitomene* (κεχαριτωμένη), meaning *"full of grace"* – (Luke 1:28), not *"highly favoured one"* as some modern English translations erroneously put it. The term "grace" does mean the favour of God, but to say that one is "full of grace" is to say that one has no room for sin. The implication of the Greek word *kecharitomene* is that Mary was gifted by God with the full measure of sanctifying grace. No more grace could be given because she was already "full," having been favoured by God more than any other human being.

According to Scripture, Mary was already in the state of grace that Christians do not attain until after they receive justification in Christ. This has led the Catholic Church to understand that God created Mary in the same state of grace as he created Adam and Eve, and that by God's mercy, Mary was not stained with original sin like the rest of us.

Theologically this is very important, because Jesus received all of his human flesh and blood from Mary. That flesh and blood ought to be unspoiled and unstained by sin. Furthermore, modern science tells us that cells from the mother and child do exchange between them during pregnancy. Jesus and Mary shared flesh and blood, as all mothers and their babies do during normal human pregnancy. That means for Jesus to inherit and maintain a perfect body from his mother, without sin, his physical mother should be without sin as well. While God can do anything he wants, it is only fitting and proper for things to be done this way, and the Scripture seems to support this with the angelic salutation "full of grace."

Some Christians believe that Mary became "without sin" when she accepted God's plan to deliver the Saviour. However, the angelic greeting seems to indicate that her state of grace existed prior to her acceptance of God's messianic plan. So while some Christians believe Mary *became* "immaculate" (without sin) at the annunciation, Catholics believe she was conceived and born "immaculate." This is what is meant by the "Immaculate Conception."[40] All Christians become immaculate (without sin) upon their baptism, which in many cases happens shortly after birth. Mary however, seems to be the only Christian who was immaculate (without sin) before her birth.

---

40 Catechism of the Catholic Church; paragraphs 490 - 493

The debate about when Mary became immaculate (without sin), or *"full of grace,"* has been long-standing in Christianity. What has not been debated, until recently, is the notion that she was not immaculate at all, indeed not *"full of grace"* but just *"highly favoured"* instead, and remained with original sin during her pregnancy with Jesus and after. That is a recent Protestant phenomenon. Such a notion was foreign to the early Church and the first Christians.

The doctrine of the Immaculate Conception of Mary is rich in ancient Jewish symbolism. It is foreshadowed in the Old Testament with the Ark of the Covenant. Hebrews 9:4 tells us that the contents contained inside the Ark of the Covenant were; the stone tablets of the Law (the word of God), along with a jar of manna (bread from heaven) and Aaron's rod (a symbol of the holy priesthood). All of these are images foreshadowing Jesus Christ, who is the incarnate Word of God (John 1:1-4,14), the Bread from Heaven (John 6:31-65) and our eternal High Priest (Hebrews 4:14).

Now the Ark of the Covenant was consecrated to God and considered holy. It was not to be touched by sinful man under penalty of death, and God himself had no problem exacting this penalty, even when a man touched it in an attempt to prevent it from falling (2nd Samuel 6:6-7; 1st Chronicles 13:9-10). This Old Testament example is designed to illustrate that the ark, which carried the symbols of the Old Covenant, was just as holy as the Old Covenant itself.

Now as I said, the stone tablets, manna and rod were signs foreshadowing Jesus Christ. He is the New Covenant. Thus the "ark" that carried him in her womb is holy too, just as the ark that carried the symbols that foreshadowed him was holy. Mary is the Ark of the New Covenant because she carried Jesus Christ in her womb. Jesus, who is the Word of God, the Bread of Life and our eternal High Priest, was carried for nine months inside the "ark" of Mary. She carried him in her arms and on her hip for another two years at least. If the ark of the Old Covenant was holy, than surely this ark of the New Covenant is even holier.

QUESTION: Do Catholics believe Mary ascended to Heaven like Jesus?

ANSWER: No. Jesus ascended to Heaven, not Mary. Mary was *assumed* into Heaven. There is a difference. The word *assumed* in this context means "taken" or "vanished," and the doctrine of the *Assumption* is deeply connected to the doctrine of the Immaculate Conception (see above). This comes directly from the Tradition of the early Church. (Remember, the "Bible Alone" doctrine is unbiblical – see Chapter 4.) Early Christians agreed universally that this happened at the end of Mary's life on earth, much in the same way Enoch (Genesis 5:24) and Elijah (2nd Kings 2:11) were assumed at the end of their lives.

Explaining that the Virgin Mary's death and entombment could not have happened without great pomp and circumstance, Epiphanius wrote in 377 AD: *"If the Holy Virgin had died and was buried, her falling asleep would have been surrounded with honour, death would have found her pure, and her crown would have been a virginal one...Had she been martyred according to what is written: 'Thine own soul a sword shall pierce', then she would shine gloriously among the martyrs, and her holy body would have been declared blessed; for by her, did light come to the world."* — (Epiphanius, Panarion, 78:23) He was just pointing out the obvious. The early Church was obsessed with relics. The slightest thread from an apostle's coat was venerated as holy by the early Christians. Had Mary not been "taken" miraculously at the end of her life, the relics of of body, hair, bones and clothing would have been venerated in churches for centuries. This did not happen. It's as if, like Christ, nothing remained of her to venerate. Like Enoch and Elijah, she just vanished. Prior to the Protestant Reformation in the sixteenth century, no Christian debated that she vanished. What was debated was whether or not she died first.

In 1950, Pope Pius XII put the debate to rest in the Catholic Church by infallibly declaring that Mary was assumed into Heaven at the end of her life.[41]

QUESTION: Why do Catholics give so much honour to Mary?

ANSWER: Throughout all of Christian history, Mary has been given the highest honour and respect. In the early Church she took on the role as the mother of all the faithful and many writings from the earliest Christians give her great respect. The real question here is why do Protestants _not_ give much honour to Mary? Mary prophesied about herself when she said: *"all generations shall call me blessed."* – (Luke 1:48) Do you call her blessed? Do you do so regularly? If not, why not? Why are you directly contradicting the Bible?

To understand Mary's blessedness, we need to understand where she stands in the Kingdom of God.

First and foremost, she is the "new Eve" in the sense that her "yes" to God (Luke 1:38) counters Eve's "no" to God (Genesis 3:2-6). Mary became the "new Eve" in the sense that she became mother of all those who trust in Jesus Christ, who is the "new Adam" (1st Corinthians 15:22 & 45), and in doing so she effectively became the first Christian. Mary was the first human being to ever believe, trust and submit to the will of God through Jesus Christ. She was the first among all Christians. That alone is enough to give her more honour than any other Christian, but it doesn't stop there.

Second, Mary gave birth to our Saviour Jesus Christ. She cared for him, fed him, nourished him, clothed him and cleaned

---

41 Catechism of the Catholic Church; paragraphs 966 & 974

him. She was our Saviour's first teacher. Can you imagine that? She was chosen to teach the Law of Moses to the one who gave us the Law of Moses. Thus the young theologian who so impressed the scribes at the Temple (Luke 2:46-47) was originally instructed in theology by her!

As if that were not enough, it doesn't stop there. Third, before the start of Jesus' ministry, Mary told others to listen and obey him (John 2:5). Thus she became the first evangelist!

Wait, there is more. Fourth, when Jesus was dying on the cross, he gave the care of his mother to his apostle Saint John. Now John was not his literal blood brother, and Jewish law would demand that the care of Jesus' mother go to the next male sibling in line. Jesus didn't do this because one didn't exist. Instead he gave the care of his mother to one of his apostles, and in so doing he made her the mother of this apostle (John 19:26-27). If Mary was made the mother of the apostle, she is by default the spiritual mother of all his disciples and of the whole Church.

Again, that should be enough, but there is more. Fifth and finally, Jesus was the King of the Jews, and because he is God incarnate, that makes him the King of kings as well. The Church is a Kingdom, in which Jesus is the King. There is however something about Jewish men that most people know. They love their mothers and they give their mothers high places of honour in their lives. Likewise, it is an ancient Jewish custom for Jewish kings to place their mothers on the throne beside them. In other words, ever since the days of Solomon (1st Kings 2:29), many Jewish kings have made their mothers (not their wives) their queens. Jesus is an unmarried Jew and he is a Jewish King. *So???* It is only natural to believe that Jesus made Mary his queen in Heaven (Revelation 12:1). The Bible says we are all made royalty in Christ (1st Peter 2:9), so it only stands to reason that Mary is all that much more so.

The honour and respect that we Catholic Christians give to Mary in no way diminishes the honour, respect and worship we give to Jesus Christ. If anything, it enhances it, because without Jesus Christ, Mary is nothing, and she would be the first one to tell us that.

CHAPTER SIX
SALVATION

QUESTION: Do Catholics believe in salvation by faith alone?

ANSWER: No! We absolutely reject this concept because the Bible specifically contradicts it. The only place in the entire Bible where the phrase "faith alone" is found is in James 2:24 which reads: *"You see that a man is justified by works and not by faith alone."*[42] There is no other passage in the Bible which suggests that "faith alone" is sufficient for salvation. There are plenty of verses that point out the superiority of faith over the old Mosaic Law (Romans 3:21-22; Romans 4:1-24; Galatians 3:16-18; Galatians 5:2-5; Ephesians 2:8-9), but none of them say that salvation comes directly by "faith alone." These passages emphasise the fact that salvation is the work of God not man. It comes to us solely by God's grace (unmerited favour and mercy toward us), and we must receive that grace as a little baby receives the care of his mother.

Saint Paul pointed out that the Law of Moses was given as a tutor (Galatians 3:24-25). It was designed to teach us that we are sinners and we need God's grace. So that when we are old enough to have faith in God's grace we may do so, not trusting in our own righteousness. It was designed to teach us that our own righteousness is insufficient and that we can't be saved on our own – neither through our faith nor works. We need God to help us. That's what the Law of Moses was all about. Father Abraham understood this, and so God initiated in his offspring (the Hebrew nation) a tutoring process (Law of Moses) that would lead that nation, and all of humanity, to the same understanding. When we receive God's grace, it produces both faith and works in us.[43] Both faith and works are the byproduct of God's grace. They go hand-

---

42 Revised Standard Version - Catholic Edition

43 Catechism of the Catholic Church; paragraphs 2001 - 2005

in-hand. As Saint James said: *"For even as the body without the spirit is dead; so also faith without works is dead."* – (James 2:26)

This is why salvation is an ongoing thing. It is a process that is not complete until we die, and this is why Saint Paul told us: *"with fear and trembling work out your salvation."* – (Philippians 2:12). You see, we Catholics believe in salvation by grace alone[44] (not faith alone), yet grace must not be resisted, either before justification, by denying the gospel (Luke 12:10), or after justification, by engaging in mortal sin (1st John 5:16).

The notion of salvation by "faith alone" came to us from the German reformer Martin Luther, as one of his "five solas" (or pillars) of German Protestant religion. It became extremely popular in the Protestant world. Luther himself could find no direct Biblical validation of this teaching, so he created one. In 1522 AD he artificially inserted the word "alone" after the word "faith" into Romans 3:23 of his German translation of the New Testament, thus changing the entire meaning of the text. Luther not only attempted to remove some books from both the Old and New Testaments (see Chapter 4), but he also had no problem changing the text of Scripture itself to suit his theological presumptions. The Catholic Church does not permit the changing of Scripture to suit theological presumptions.

As Catholics we do not believe we "earn" our way to heaven as if we did not need the merits of Christ. Far from it! We believe that everything we have comes directly from the grace of God, and this includes our salvation, our faith *and* our works.

QUESTION: Do Catholics believe in "once saved, always saved?"

---

44 Catechism of the Catholic Church; paragraphs 1996 - 2000

ANSWER: No. The Scriptures are clear that one can lose his salvation if one rejects the forgiveness of God, either by persisting in unbelief or else persisting in mortal sin without repentance. (Matthew 7:21; Matthew 24:13; Romans 11:22; 1st Corinthians 9:27; 1st Corinthians 10:11-12; 2nd Corinthians 11:15; Galatians 5:4; 2nd Timothy 2:11-13; Hebrews 6:4-6; Hebrews 10:26-27; Philemon 2:12; 1st Peter 1:9; Revelation 20:12-13)

QUESTION: Why do Catholics baptise babies when they can't even understand what is going on?

ANSWER: We Catholics baptise our infant children because Jesus said: *"Suffer the little children, and forbid them not to come to me: for the kingdom of heaven is for such."* – (Matthew 19:14) Saint Peter told us that salvation comes through baptism (1st Peter 3:21). We also baptise them because Saint Paul has specifically told us that baptism replaces circumcision as our initiation into covenant with God (Colossians 2:11-12). Jews circumcise their boys at eight days of age, to initiate them into the covenant God made with Moses. God didn't have a problem bringing babies into his covenant of the Law? Why would he have a problem bringing babies into his covenant of Grace?

As pointed out above, we Catholics do not believe in salvation by "faith alone," so faith is not necessary to receive God's grace when one is too young to understand or believe. An infant child just receives, and this is the example God wants all of his followers to understand about how salvation works. It's totally God's doing not ours! We are expected to participate in our salvation (by faith and works) when we are old enough to do so, but it is neither our "faith alone" nor our "works alone" that saves us. Nor is it our "faith plus works" that saves us. It is God's grace and God's grace alone – period. There is no better example than that of an infant child receiving the sacrament of baptism to illustrate this.

The child can do nothing, neither believe nor work. All the child can do is receive God's grace, and so that is what the child does.[45] That is what we must understand. God is our salvation – not us.

The early Christians baptised their infants and children and we have record of this going back as far as the second century AD. The notion that children should not be baptised, because they are not old enough to express faith, did not come about until after the Protestant Reformation in the sixteenth century, and probably derives from the false notion that salvation comes through "faith alone." Indeed, if salvation came through "faith alone" then there would be no way anyone too young to express faith could be saved, or initiated into God's covenant made through Jesus Christ. So it would be wrong to baptise them. Thus, according to some Protestant rationale, babies who die in infancy would have no assurance of salvation whatsoever, since they would not have ever attained an age in which they can express faith. Again, this is probably the result of the "faith alone" misunderstanding. Because of this, many Protestants have come up with the "age of reason" idea to answer the unsettling thought that God would send unbaptised and unbelieving children to hell. For this reason, a few Protestants have even rejected the idea of original sin altogether.

These notions however, have no basis in Scripture. Since we know that salvation does not come by "faith alone" (see above), then we know that the covenant of salvation in Christ can certainly be presented to an infant through baptism, or a child of any age, just as the covenant of the Law in Moses was presented to infant males through circumcision. The Catholic message on baptism is the same as the Jewish message on circumcision. Don't wait! Initiate your children into God's covenant as quickly as possible, both for their benefit and yours.[46]

---

45 Catechism of the Catholic Church; paragraph 1216, 1250 - 1252

46 Catechism of the Catholic Church; paragraph 1250

QUESTION: Why do Catholics believe in Purgatory as a place in between Heaven and Hell?

ANSWER: Actually Catholics don't believe that, and the Church doesn't teach that. In spite of all the myth and speculation that swirls around the topic of Purgatory, the Church only officially teaches two things about it.[47] One, it exists (Matthew 5:26; Matthew 12:32; 1st Peter 3:18-20 & 4:6). Two, our prayers and sacrifices help those who go there (2nd Maccabees 12:44-46; 1st Corinthians 15:29-30; 2nd Timothy 1:16-18). Now beyond that it's just a matter of explaining what it is.

Explanations have changed a bit over the centuries as societies understand things in different ways, just as explanations of Heaven and Hell have changed over the centuries too. The first thing we need to understand about Purgatory is that it's not an "in between" state of Heaven and Hell. Quite the opposite is true actually. Purgatory is connected to Heaven in some sense. Some might even call it *"Heaven's Front Door."* The only people who go to Purgatory are people who are already saved, and the reason why they go to Purgatory (or more accurately "through" Purgatory), on their way to Heaven, is to let the merits of Christ's atoning sacrifice burn away all of their sinful attachments to this present world (1st Corinthians 3:11-15). This is so all that which is pure and holy in their lives may shine more brightly in the glory of Heaven. That's basically it. It is the final method through which God takes imperfect people at the end of their lives, and through the merits of Christ, transforms them into perfect and glorified Saints in Heaven.

QUESTION: Do Catholics believe Protestants can be saved?

ANSWER: The answer is essentially yes. You see, Catholics and Protestants are united together by virtue of their common

---

47 Catechism of the Catholic Church; paragraphs 1030 - 1032

baptism in the name of the Trinity.[48] Every baptism performed in the name of the Holy Trinity – Father, Son and Holy Spirit – is essentially a Catholic baptism, and every Protestant church performs baptism this way. So that means that every baptised Protestant has essentially received a Catholic baptism, regardless of who performed it or where it was performed, and the Catholic Church fully recognises this. This is why the Catholic Church does not attempt to "re-baptise" Protestant converts.

So right from the start, Protestants are initiated into the New Covenant of salvation in Jesus Christ in a fully Catholic way. After that, things start to change of course. Protestants have their own beliefs and practises which range far and wide, depending on which denomination or affiliation we are talking about.

The Catholic Church teaches that *"there is no salvation outside of the Church"*[49] and by this it means sacramental membership through baptism, not necessarily official membership on paper. The Catholic Church also recognises the gifts of the Holy Spirit operating within Protestant churches, and officially considers Protestants to be "fellow Christians" by virtue of their Trinitarian baptism.[50]

Where Protestants enter a precarious position is when it comes to their knowledge of the Catholic Church. Those who are ignorant of the Catholic Church's essential role in salvation history cannot be held accountable for what they do not know. However, those who have studied history, and the teachings of the Catholic Church, knowing full well the essential role the Catholic Church plays in salvation history, will be held accountable for what they know.[51] It is a cause for fear and trembling before God Almighty.

48 Catechism of the Catholic Church; paragraphs 818 - 819

49 Catechism of the Catholic Church; paragraph 846

50 Catechism of the Catholic Church; paragraph 1271

51 Catechism of the Catholic Church; paragraph 846

With knowledge comes responsibility. Protestants who have studied and know the truth about Catholicism, must for the sake of their immortal souls, seek reconciliation with the Catholic Church. We all must follow the convictions of a well-informed conscience.

CHAPTER SEVEN
THE SACRAMENT

QUESTION: Do Catholics really believe that communion bread and wine become the literal flesh and blood of Jesus Christ?

ANSWER: Yes, because Jesus said so. Have you ever read John 6:66? In addition to the apocalyptic connection to this number, it's the most frightening verse in the whole Bible. It says: *"Because of this many of his disciples turned back and no longer went about with him."* — (John 6:66)[52] What was the context of this passage? Jesus just completed his explanation of the mystery of Holy Communion to his disciples (John 6:51-65). He described himself as the *"bread of life,"* and just when you think Jesus was pulling one of those non-literal parables again, he kicks it up a notch and goes straight into literal speech. He tells his disciples that they must literally *"eat"* his flesh and *"drink"* his blood to have eternal life. Jesus tells his disciples that this is spiritual (as in not carnal) but that it is literal too. Read these passages over and over again to see for yourself. Many of his disciples left him after this. He didn't go after them and say: *"Wait! I wasn't speaking literally. You misunderstood."* It would be cruel to suggest that Jesus was deliberately misleading his disciples to drive them away with a symbolic parable that he allowed them to misunderstand as literal. No. Jesus Christ was speaking literally here, and he was allowing his own disciples to leave him because of it.

Now since the earliest days of Christianity, well documented all the way back to the early second century, the Church has always taught that when the priest consecrates the communion bread and wine, these elements literally become the body and blood of Jesus Christ hidden supernaturally under the *physical appearance* of bread

---

52 Revised Standard Version - Catholic Edition

and wine.[53] Saint Ignatius of Antioch, writing in about 105 AD, said the following about those who did not believe this to be literal: *"Heretics abstain from the Eucharist and from prayer, because they do not confess that the Eucharist is the flesh of our Saviour Jesus Christ."* – (Letter to the Smyrnaeans 6) This same Ignatius, who was the Bishop of Antioch and ordained by the Apostle John, was shortly thereafter martyred in the circus in Rome where he was fed to lions before a cheering crowd.

When we say the bread and wine literally become the body and blood of Jesus Christ, what we mean to say is that both species contain all of the properties of Jesus Christ. The bread literally becomes the body of Jesus Christ. The wine literally becomes the blood. Now, Jesus Christ is living, and therefore his body and blood cannot be separated. So to partake of just one species is to partake of the whole and complete Christ[54] – body and blood, humanity, together with his soul and divinity.[55] When we look at the Biblical passages dealing with communion (Matthew 26:26-28; Mark 14:22-24; Luke 22:19-20; 1st Corinthians 10:16; 1st Corinthians 11:23-29), not a single one suggests a non-literal interpretation is in order. Not a single one gives us a "symbolic" or "metaphorical" context. It is all very literal and straightforward. Remember, the first rule of Biblical interpretation is the Rule of Context, which states that "context rules!"

QUESTION: So does this mean that Catholics believe Jesus is re-crucified or re-slain every time a priest says the mass?

ANSWER: No. We believe the Eucharist is the living and resurrected Christ that is made present to us,[56] who was once

---

53 Catechism of the Catholic Church; paragraphs 1375 - 1376

54 Catechism of the Catholic Church; paragraph 1390

55 Catechism of the Catholic Church; paragraph 1374

56 Catechism of the Catholic Church; paragraph 1373

crucified, once and for all time,[57] not to be misunderstood as to say that Christ is somehow re-sacrificed, re-crucified, re-killed or re-murdered every time we celebrate the Holy Mass.[58] That would be both blasphemy and nonsense. No, the communion we receive is the living and resurrected Jesus Christ who was slain once, resurrected and now shares himself supernaturally with us. The sacrifice was offered (slain) 2,000 years ago, but has been re-presented and consumed ever since.

QUESTION: Do Catholics believe Protestant communion is the same as Catholic communion?

ANSWER: No. This is because we believe the authority to ask God to bring about the transubstantiation of the communion elements was given by Jesus Christ to his apostles, who in turn gave it to the bishops and priests they chose. This authority is passed down through generations in a specific and defined line of succession which can be easily traced through history back to the apostles. In order for a transubstantiation of the communion elements to occur, a minister must be properly ordained by a bishop who has this authentic apostolic succession back to the apostles. Protestant ministers generally do not have this, and most would not dare to claim it, so they cannot call on God for transubstantiation of the communion elements. So for most Protestants, communion means something altogether different than for Catholics.

QUESTION: So then is Protestant communion just symbolic?

ANSWER: For most Protestants, when they celebrate communion, it really is just a symbolic meal of remembrance, similar to the Jewish Passover Seder. While there are a few

---

57 Catechism of the Catholic Church; paragraph 1366

58 Catechism of the Catholic Church; paragraph 1545

Protestant ministers here and there (perhaps some Anglicans and Scandinavian Lutherans) who may actually have legitimate apostolic succession, the overwhelming vast majority of Protestant ministers do not, nor do they claim to have it. So for them, nothing really happens at the consecration portion of the service, assuming the communion elements are consecrated at all. In some Protestant churches they are not.

Because of this, some Protestant churches put the emphasis on everyone in the congregation receiving the communion elements at the exact same time. This is their understanding of "communion." Thus, the bread and wine (often grape juice) are distributed in small plastic cups in advance, while everyone waits for the pastor to give the cue. At that moment all receive the elements together simultaneously, as they communally remember the last supper of Jesus Christ.

This is considerably different from the Catholic practise of Holy Communion which we understand to be literal. In Catholic churches the emphasis is on the individual reception of the real presence of God in the communion elements. The word "communion" then takes on a much deeper meaning, in that the communicant is literally having physical contact with God the Son – Jesus Christ – under the accidental appearance of bread and wine.

QUESTION: So if Catholics believe the communion elements are literally the manifestation of Jesus Christ, who is God, does that mean that Catholics worship these communion elements as God?

ANSWER: Yes.[59]

---

59 Catechism of the Catholic Church; paragraphs 1378 & 1418

QUESTION: How is the Catholic worship of bread and wine not idolatry?

ANSWER: Well, if it were only "bread and wine," then it really would be idolatry, but it's not merely "bread and wine." It is the real and literal presence of Jesus Christ (God the Son) made manifest under the accidental appearance of bread and wine. So when Catholics worship this Holy Eucharist we are worshipping the literal and physical presence of Jesus Christ. Many Catholics, myself included, whisper the words of Saint Thomas at the consecration and elevation of the communion elements: *"My Lord, and my God."* – (John 20:28) It is fitting that these words came from "doubting Thomas" when he finally realised the truth and believed. Every Catholic, especially a Protestant convert like myself, has this Thomistic epiphany when he finally realises what Jesus was talking about in John 6:51-65. This communion Eucharist, which just looks like ordinary bread and wine, really and truly is the risen Lord Jesus Christ! You see, it's just a matter of taking Jesus at his word. He said it, I believe it, and that settles it. The real question here is; if he said it, and you don't believe it, why not?

QUESTION: How can this Catholic worship of communion elements be Biblical?

ANSWER: Worship usually involves sacrifice. It has always involved sacrifice since the first recorded act of worship in the Bible (Genesis 4:4). Under the Old Covenant, unblemished animals were brought to the Temple for sacrifice (Leviticus 1:1 *through* Leviticus 9:24), and ancient Jews would worship God as these animals were being sacrificed to him. Then, especially during the Passover sacrifice, the meat from this animal holocaust was given back to the Jewish worshipper, and roasted in fire for consumption in the Passover Seder meal. Thus, every Jewish sacrifice had two parts, the offering and the consumption. The offering happened only once, when the animal was killed. The consumption happened multiple times, as the worshipper ate the Passover lamb, one bite after another, sharing it with others in his family, and then going back for seconds and thirds, until all of the meat was gone (Exodus 12:1-11; Numbers 9:9-13).

This illustrates communion in the Catholic understanding of Jesus Christ as God's Passover Lamb. The offering of this sacrifice of Christ happened only once, on the cross at Calvary. The consumption happens many times, millions of times actually, in Eucharistic liturgies all over the globe, for century after century, until this present day. However, like the loaves of bread and fish that were multiplied in the gospels (Matthew 14:13-21), this sacrificial consumption never runs out. Miraculously, it continues indefinitely until the end of time when all have been filled with the physical presence of Jesus Christ.

As stated above, true worship usually involves a sacrifice combined with adoration – the complete submission of the body, mind, soul and will. This is what Catholics are doing in the holy liturgy of the mass. This is worship in a Biblical sense. Prayer by itself is not worship. Praise and song by themselves are not worship. However, when these things are combined with a real "flesh and blood" sacrifice, and the full submission of our bodies, minds, souls and will, we have authentic Biblical worship, which is identical to that of the Hebrew Patriarchs, ancient Israel and the early Church.

QUESTION: How can any reasonable and sane person be expected to believe such absurdity as the transubstantiation of bread and wine into the literal flesh and blood of Jesus Christ?

ANSWER: Remember John 6:66? From the very beginning, many have left the company of Jesus and his apostles over this teaching. When you really stop and think about it, taking Jesus' words at face value over the transubstantiation is no more absurd than many of the other miracles the Bible records. Do you believe Moses parted the Red Sea? Do you believe God stopped the sun for Joshua? Do you believe Jonah was swallowed and vomited by a giant fish? Do you believe Jesus walked on water? Do you believe Jesus healed the sick and raised the dead? Do you believe that he himself rose from the dead and ascended into heaven? If you can believe such "absurd" things as these, how hard can it be to believe a properly consecrated Eucharist (communion bread and wine) is the literal flesh and blood of Jesus Christ? Especially since he said it is.

CHAPTER EIGHT
THE CHURCH

QUESTION: Do Catholics really believe the Catholic Church is the one and only Church ever established by Jesus Christ?

ANSWER: Yes, we most certainly do. This is based both on the Biblical record and historical evidence. The term "Catholic" is Greek – *katholikos* (καθολικός) – and means "whole, universal and complete." The term "Catholic Church" has been used since the late first century to contrast the Church of the apostles with false heretical sects that were springing up among the Greek Gnostics.

In 105 AD, Saint Ignatius of Antioch wrote the following to the Christians in Smyrnea: *"See that you all follow the bishop, even as Jesus Christ does the Father, and the presbytery* [priests] *as you would the apostles; and reverence the deacons, as being the institution of God. Let no man do anything connected with the Church without the bishop. Let that be deemed a proper Eucharist, which is* [administered] *either by the bishop, or by one to whom he has entrusted it. Wherever the bishop shall appear, there let the multitude also be; even as, wherever Jesus Christ is, there is the Catholic Church."* — (Epistle of Ignatius to the Smyrnaeans 8) Now this Ignatius of Antioch was a bishop in the early Church who was ordained by the Apostle John himself.

We believe the Catholic Church is the messianic Kingdom of God, promised to ancient Israel, and is indeed the heir of ancient Israel.[60] In fact, in the Greek version of the Old Testament (Septuagint), ancient Israel is referred to many times as *ecclesia* (ἐκκλησία) or "the Church." The New Testament Church (ecclesia) is just a continuation of that. Jesus Christ is the King of Israel, and therefore the King of the Catholic Church. This Kingdom/Church was established between 30 - 33 AD, when King Jesus made Peter

---

60 Catechism of the Catholic Church; paragraphs 751, 761-766 & 877

his prime minister: *"Simon Peter answered and said: Thou art Christ, the Son of the living God. And Jesus answering, said to him: Blessed art thou, Simon Bar-Jona: because flesh and blood hath not revealed it to thee, but my Father who is in heaven. And I say to thee: That thou art Peter; and upon this rock I will build my church, and the gates of hell shall not prevail against it. And I will give to thee the keys of the kingdom of heaven. And whatsoever thou shalt bind upon earth, it shall be bound also in heaven: and whatsoever thou shalt loose upon earth, it shall be loosed also in heaven."* — (Matthew 16:16-19) Ever since then, this Catholic Church has been established, and it was inaugurated at the Feast of Pentecost following the death and resurrection of Jesus Christ.

At this point the leadership of ancient Israel ceased to be the scribes, priests and pharisees. From that time forward, the true and authentic leadership of Israel was the apostles appointed by King Jesus. Historical records tell us that in about 42 AD,[61] the King's prime minister (Saint Peter) travelled from Antioch to Rome, and there he established his permanent *Apostolic See* (meaning a seat of authority). It was at this time the Catholic Church became the "Roman Catholic Church" because Peter was now in Rome. Later, Saint Paul arrived in Rome, and together the two built the Roman Catholic Church into the headquarters of all ancient Christianity. Peter and Paul were martyred in Rome in about the year 67 AD. Paul was beheaded and Peter was crucified upside-down. Since then, Peter's direct successors have carried on the ministry of Saint Peter, having inherited through ordination and consecration the same apostolic authority once held by Saint Peter.

QUESTION: So do Catholics believe Protestant churches are illegitimate?

---

61 Irenaeus, Against Heresies, 3:1:1 (circa 180 AD); Eusebius of Caesarea, The Chronicle (circa 303 AD)

ANSWER: That depends on what you mean by the word "churches." Catholics believe that Jesus Christ established only one Church – the Catholic Church – but the word "church" is used many ways in the English language. It could refer to the whole company of Christian believers around the world. It could refer to a small group of Christian believers in a local area. Or it could refer to an actual chapel structure in which Christian worship is celebrated. All of these are legitimate uses of the word "church" in the English language.

Now, when it comes to how these churches were established, that's a totally different matter. Catholics understand Jesus as having established one institutional Church upon Peter (the "rock") and that this institutional Church subsists entirely in those local churches, around the world, in full-communion with the successor of Saint Peter (the "Patriarch of Rome" or the "Pope"). This One, Holy, Catholic and Apostolic Church is considered whole and complete in and of itself.[62]

Now, that being said, the Catholic Church does fully acknowledge the presence of Christians outside this institutional structure, who may be united to it through the sacrament of Trinitarian baptism,[63] but for whatever reasons have been separated (in diaspora) from visible union with the pope. Likewise, these Christians have, in many cases, organised themselves into their own visible communities wherein the gifts of the Holy Spirit are clearly in operation. The Holy Spirit uses these communities as a means of salvation, but they derive their power from the fullness of grace that Jesus Christ gave to the Catholic Church.[64] It is their connection to Catholic truth that makes them a means of grace for the salvation of souls.

---

62 Catechism of the Catholic Church; paragraph 820

63 Catechism of the Catholic Church; paragraph 818

64 Catechism of the Catholic Church; paragraph 819

From the very beginning, men have taken it upon themselves to call upon the name of Jesus outside of the institutional Church Jesus established. While this has never been ideal, Jesus likewise did not condemn them for it (Mark 9:38-41), especially if they did not know any better. If anything, the operation of the Holy Spirit in these other communities is a call for Catholic unity among Christians, and indeed that was the desire of Christ all along. For he plainly told his apostles, on the night before he died, that any lack of Catholic unity among Christians would be a scandal and a hindrance to effective evangelism of the unsaved (John 17:20-21).

These non-catholic Christian communities may not have been established by Jesus Christ, therefore they are not "The Church" in the proper understanding of the word, but they can nevertheless be "a church" or "churches" in a local sense, and in a linguistic sense, so as to say real Christian "communities." So while it would be improper to call these churches "illegitimate," because they are clearly legitimate gatherings of Christians, it is only fair and honest to understand that they are not the institutional "Church" established by Jesus Christ in 33 AD.

QUESTION: How can Catholics say that Peter is the "rock" upon which Jesus built the Church, when clearly the passage used to support this uses two completely different words for "rock?"

ANSWER: In Matthew 16, the Greek word used for Peter is *petros* (πέτρος) while the Greek word used for the rock Jesus said he would build his Church on is *petra* (πέτρᾳ). These are two completely different words. "Petros" means little stone, while "petra" means huge boulder. "*And I say to thee: That thou art* [Petros]; *and upon this* [petra] *I will build my church*" – (Matthew 16:18).

84

The problem here is the Greek language. You see, in Greek, words are inflected with gender. So "petros" is inflected with a male gender, while "petra" is inflected with a female gender. We see similar gender inflection in many other languages too. Now because these two Greek words have a different gender, and because they mean two different things, it has led many Protestant theologians to teach that while Jesus gave the name "rock" *petros* (πέτρος) to Simon Bar-Jona, he did so symbolically, because he was *really* talking about a completely different symbolic "rock" *petra* (πέτρα) which they say was the revelation that Simon gave – that Jesus is the messianic Son of God. The problem with this interpretation is that it's linguistically impossible and out of context. These Protestant theologians have fallen victim to the old language trap.

The Greek version of the Gospel of Matthew is a translation from an original Aramaic text. One of the early Church Fathers, Irenaeus, wrote the following in about 180 AD: "*Matthew also issued a written Gospel among the Hebrews <u>in their own dialect</u>, while Peter and Paul were preaching at Rome. and laying the foundations of the Church.*" — (Against Heresies 3:1) What was the dialect of the Hebrews during that time? It was Aramaic. So based on Irenaeus' testimony, we know the first (and original) version of Matthew's gospel was written in Aramaic not Greek. So what many Protestants are relying upon to make their argument that Peter is not the rock is actually a translation of Matthew's text, not the original text itself.

The Greek translator of this Aramaic text ran into a problem with the Aramaic word for "rock" in reference to the name Jesus gave to Simon. The obvious Greek translation for the "rock" upon which Jesus would build his Church is *petra*, meaning a large boulder, but the problem is that in Greek, Petra is a girl's name! You can't give Peter a girl's name!!! The masculine form *petros* works as a proper boy's name, but means "little stone" and doesn't convey the massive character of the "rock" that Jesus built his Church on. The Greek translator of Matthew's gospel was simply trying to make Matthew's plain Aramaic statement, about Peter being the "rock," work in the Greek language.

The truth is, Jesus didn't name Simon "Petros" at all! In fact, there is no evidence that Jesus ever even spoke the Greek word *petros*. Jesus was a Jew who lived in Galilee of Palestine. He spoke Aramaic, as all Jews did at that time, with perhaps a smattering of Hebrew, which was at that time nearly an extinct language, spoken exclusively in the Temple in Jerusalem. However, Hebrew would not be the language Jesus would speak in public settings. Instead he would use Aramaic, because that is what everyone else would understand, and if Saint Matthew's intended audience for his written gospel was the Jews (as every Biblical scholar affirms) then of course he would write it in Aramaic. The majority of the world's Jewish population was living in Palestine at that time, and they spoke Aramaic not Greek. It is very clear, based on both tradition and history, that the name Jesus gave to Simon Bar-Jonah was not the Greek word for rock (Petros) but rather the Aramaic word for rock *cephas* (Aramaic: כיפא, or Greek version: Κηφας), and this is backed with Scripture (John 1:42; 1st Corinthians 1:12; 1st Corinthians 15:5; Galatians 2:9; etc.). Now the Aramaic word *cephas* means "rock." It neither means big rock nor little rock, and it is neither male nor female. It just means "rock." In Aramaic, Jesus would have said: *"And I say to thee: That thou art* [Cephas]*; and upon this* [cephas] *I will build my church"* – (Matthew 16:18). It's really very simple you see, and it's contextual, because of what Jesus said in his next breath: *"And I will give to thee the keys of the kingdom of heaven. And whatsoever thou shalt bind upon earth, it shall be bound also in heaven: and whatsoever thou shalt loose upon earth, it shall be loosed also in heaven."* – (Matthew 16:19)

What did Jesus do here? Simple. He gave Peter (Cephas) the promise of authority, real spiritual authority, the authority to "bind and loose" meaning the authority to make doctrine and law within the Church which will be backed by the forces of Heaven itself! Jesus was doing what every king always does. He was investing authority into his prime minister. In the Old Testament we see a similar pattern, with similar terminology, wherein King Hezekiah appointed Eliakim as his prime minister using a "key" as a symbol of his authority (Isaiah 22:20-22). Here, in Matthew's gospel, King Jesus is doing the same. A Jewish audience, in first century Palestine, would have immediately picked up on this.

QUESTION: How can Peter (Cephas) be the "rock" when the Apostle Paul calls Jesus Christ the "rock?"

ANSWER: Saint Paul the Apostle refers to Jesus Christ as the "rock" in 1st Corinthians 10:4 which says: *"And all drank the same spiritual drink; (and they drank of the spiritual rock that followed them, and the rock was Christ.)"* – (1st Corinthians 10:4) He even uses the feminine Greek word *petra* (πέτρᾳ) to do this. However, this is easily answered in the historical fact that Paul wrote his epistles in Greek. Unlike Matthew's gospel, he did not originally write in Aramaic. The most commonly used words for "rock" available in Greek were *petra* (πέτρᾳ) and *petros* (πέτρος). So Paul used the feminine word *petra* (πέτρᾳ), meaning "large boulder," to describe Jesus Christ in a spiritual sense. Notice he did not name Jesus "Petra." That would be disrespectful and blasphemous to give the Son of God a girl's name. He just used the word to describe him spiritually. There are other similar references to God in both the Old and New Testaments. They are completely unrelated to Matthew 16:18, which was originally written in Aramaic, wherein Jesus actually renamed Simon to "Cephas" (Aramaic: כיפא), meaning "rock," and said he would build his Church upon this "Cephas."

QUESTION: How can Catholics say Peter died in Rome, when there is no Biblical record of Peter ever being in Rome?

ANSWER: Just because it's not written plainly in the Book of Acts doesn't mean it didn't happen. It is astonishing that so many modern Protestants assert this when the historical records are indisputable, and no early Christian writing even questions that Peter and Paul died in Rome.

For example; Saint Ignatius of Antioch, on his journey to be martyred in Rome in 105 AD, wrote to the Roman Christians, urging them not to lobby for his release, saying: *"I issue you no commands, like Peter and Paul: they were Apostles, while I am but a captive."* – (Epistle to the Romans 4). Thus he indicated the position of authority Peter and Paul held in Rome during their residence there. Irenaeus, in about 180 AD, summarised the position of the early Roman Church in ancient Christianity as follows: *"the very great, the very ancient, and universally known Church founded and organised at Rome by the two most glorious apostles, Peter and Paul; as also the faith preached to men, which comes down to our time by means of the successions of the bishops. For it is a matter of necessity that every Church should agree with this Church, on account of its preeminent authority, that is, the faithful everywhere, inasmuch as the tradition has been preserved continuously by those who exist everywhere."* – (Irenaeus, Against Heresies 3:2) This is just but a small example of the writings of the ancients who universally asserted, and never denied, the presence of Peter and Paul in Rome, and even more so, asserted that because of their presence in Rome, the Roman Church had a position of preeminence in the ancient world.

However, in addition to that, it is a mistake to say that there is no Biblical record of Peter ever living in Rome. Indeed there is. The Bible contains one of the letters written by Saint Peter to the Christians in Asia Minor. Here it would appear that Peter was writing to some of the Christians he once shepherded in that area. At the end of this short epistle he sends his farewell: *"The church that is in Babylon, elected together with you, saluteth you: and so doth my son Mark."* – (1st Peter 5:13) The reference to Mark as a "son" again demonstrates the paternal nature of Christian leaders as "fathers" in the early Church (see Chapter 3). Indeed, what else could Mark call Peter but "Father?" The only question that remains is: "Where is Babylon?" It's certainly not the literal Babylon in present day Iraq. During Saint Peter's time this literal Babylon in Iraq was a ghost town that was only very sparsely populated. There is no record of Saint Peter ever going there and indeed there would be no reason why he would. Peter's apostolic journey led him out of Jerusalem up north to Galilee, and then further north and west to Antioch. Finally, he settled in "Babylon," which is nowhere to be found in Asia Minor. However, the ancient Christians did refer to Rome as "spiritual Babylon." Pagan Rome was the only ancient city that Scripture refers to as "Babylon" (Revelation 17:5). Could this be what Saint Peter meant in his closing farewell to the Christians of Asia Minor? This is the most likely explanation, and one that perfectly fits with the historical record. Peter was writing from "spiritual Babylon" (Pagan Rome) to Christians he used to shepherd himself in Asia Minor. Yes, Peter was in Rome. He lived there for about 25 years (AD 42-67)[65] and he established his apostolic headquarters there, bestowing his full apostolic authority upon his successors.

QUESTION: Maybe Jesus did invest his authority into his apostles, but does that mean these apostles could really transfer that authority on to their successors?

ANSWER: Let me rephrase this question. What is really being asked here is: *"Did the apostles have the authority to vest others with the same authority Jesus gave them?"* Let's look at what Scripture has to say about that. After the ascension of Jesus into heaven, while the

---

65 Eusebius, Church History, 2, 14, 5 (circa 325 AD)

apostles were waiting in the upper room for the feast of Pentecost to come and give them the power of the Holy Spirit, they decided amongst themselves who among the one-hundred and twenty lesser disciples would replace Judas Iscariot (the fallen apostle). They settled on Matthias and vested him with the full authority of an apostle, completely replacing the office that Judas abandoned (Acts 1:15-26). It was as if Jesus himself had ordained and consecrated him. So we know the apostles had the authority to transfer their full apostolic authority on to others. We know the process through which this is done by the laying on of hands (1st Timothy 4:4 & 5:22). We have historical records that plainly lay out this apostolic succession from many of the apostles to modern times. No such record is more clearly documented than that of Saint Peter. So did the apostles have the authority to transfer their same authority on to others? Yes! Absolutely! There is no logical or Biblical reason to doubt this. The direct successors of the apostles are the bishops of the Catholic Church.

QUESTION: Why do we need apostolic successors when we have the Bible?

ANSWER: It is wonderful that we have the Bible today, but let us remember that the only reason why we have the Bible (in one complete volume) is because of the work of these apostolic successors (bishops) in the late 4th century. We also must remember that the Bible was never intended to be a catechism of systematic theology. It is a cross-section of Christian history and Tradition. It is not a concise encyclopaedia of it. We also have to remember what the Bible itself says about the bishops, specifically instructing us to follow their teaching (1st Corinthians 16:15-16; 1st Thessalonians 5:12; Hebrews 13:17), and how it calls the Church (not the Bible) "*the pillar and ground of the truth*" — (1st Timothy 3:15).

QUESTION: How can the Catholic Church really be the Church Jesus established when there are scandals and corruption?

ANSWER: This is a fair question. Before I answer it however, I should point out that much of the historical record concerning scandals and corruption in the Church is tainted by those who wrote the history. In predominately Protestant countries, like the United States for example, history is told in such a way that often favours Protestant churches over the Catholic Church.

Case in point, after years of critical review, we now know that much of the stories we were told about the inquisitions were untrue. While abuses obviously did happen, a good portion of what most people commonly hear was made up propaganda put out by the English crown (which was Protestant) to defame the Catholic Church and bolster the Protestant Church of England.

We know now that much of what we are told about the crusades is only half of the story. The crusades were actually a military retaliation for hundreds of years of Islamic jihad against Christianity, much in the same way the United States retaliated against al-Qaeda and the Taliban after the 9-11 attacks in 2001 AD.

We now know more about the details of the Galileo affair, in which we've learned that Galileo was tried for heresy because he attempted to reinterpret the Bible, not because he taught the heliocentric theory on the motion of planets. (That theory was also taught by many priests and professors in universities at the time who faced no such inquisition.)

Further investigation into the World War II records of Pope Pius XII reveal that he did more to help European Jews escape Nazi persecution than any other world leader at the time, and that no real and substantial cooperation ever existed between the Third Reich and the Holy See. Furthermore, evidence has surfaced that

Hitler actually tried to have Pope Pius XII kidnapped multiple times.

Finally, a detailed investigation into the recent sexual abuse scandals in the Catholic Church has revealed that less than 5% of all clergy were involved in this, either directly or through coverup. While this statistic is painfully high, it is no higher than the statistic of similar sexual abuse cases found in <u>all other churches and denominations</u>. (Let us never forget the 95% of good Catholic and Protestant clergy who had nothing to do with this!) It is also significantly lower, many times lower, than the type of sexual abuse of minors that is often found in secular (non-religious) institutions, such as public schools for example. The United States Department of Education commissioned educational researcher Charol Shakeshaft to investigate the incidence of sexual abuse and coverup in America's public schools. The "Educator Sexual Misconduct" report was the first of its kind and a watershed event in this field of research. According to a 2006 National Review Online opinion column, Shakeshaft said: *"the physical sexual abuse of students in* [public] *schools is likely more than 100 times the abuse by* [Catholic] *priests."*

So the point I'm making here is that while scandal and corruption are a real part of Church history, it is often the case that these things get exaggerated either for government propaganda reasons, or for reasons of sensationalist journalism. Scandals and corruption are real. The sensational exaggeration that surrounds them is often not real.

So with that being said, are we to believe that the Church Jesus Christ established would be free of scandal and corruption? Let's take a look at ancient Israel before Christ. We know that the priests of ancient Israel once offered child sacrifices (Jeremiah 32:32-35). We know that a cult of Pagan prostitutes once inhabited the Temple of the Lord in Jerusalem (2nd Kings 23:7). Did this change the identity of ancient Israel? Did Israel cease to be Israel when these things happened? No. Israel remained Israel. Nobody went out and tried to start a "another Israel" somewhere else. Scandals and corruption were just part of the game. That's what happens when you put human beings in charge of things. In spite of this, Saint John the Apostle wrote that *"salvation is of the Jews"* – (John 4:22).

Would Jesus' Church then be free of such corruption? Don't tell Jesus that, for he (knowingly of course) appointed the worst form of thief and traitor (Judas Iscariot) right into the highest levels of management within the Church at its most embryonic stage! (Mark 14:43-46) Then of course, we have the cowardice of Saint Peter, King Jesus' own prime minister (Mark 14:66-72). Later we see the hypocrisy of this same prime minister in Antioch (Galatians 2:11-21). All of this is typical and expected. This is what happens when human beings are put in charge of things. The Church did not cease to be the Church at this point. Nobody went out and tried to start "another Church" because the old Church was too corrupt. Nobody can reform an organisation from the outside.

Through all of this, the Catholic Church retained her identity as the *"Israel of God"* – (Galatians 6:16). For the Bible tells us that in spite of man's unfaithfulness, God remains faithful to the people and institutions he established (Romans 3:3-4 & 2nd Timothy 2:13). Jesus himself warned us that this would happen when he told us about the parable of the weeds and the wheat (Matthew 13:24-30), and the parable of the net that collects both good fish and bad fish (Matthew 13:47-48). This is what it means to be part of an institution established by God but run by men. The occasional infidelity of the Church's leaders does not in any way nullify the Church's message of the gospel, nor does it in any way alter its identity as the Kingdom of God, the "New Israel"

(Galatians 6:15-16)[66] and the one Catholic Church established by Jesus Christ.

QUESTION: Do Catholics really believe the pope is infallible?

ANSWER: Actually it's worse than that. We believe that we are infallible sometimes too. You see, sometimes we Catholics make simple arithmetic statements like: one plus one equals two. That's an infallible statement! You see it is totally accurate and "without error."

To understand we must define what is meant by the word "infallible." Contrary to popular belief, it does not mean sinlessness. The pope can sin, and indeed many popes have sinned, starting with the first one (Saint Peter) when he denied our Lord three times (John 18:15-27), and then later when he hypocritically denied the power of the gospel to reconcile Jewish and Gentile believers in Christ (Galatians 2:11-21). Nor does infallibility mean the pope can't make a mistake in his regular teachings or administrative acts.

What the doctrine of papal infallibility means is the pope is protected from error by the Holy Spirit himself, when he dogmatically defines doctrine from the Chair of Saint Peter.[67] In other words, when he is exercising his "binding and loosing authority" (Matthew 16:19) as Saint Peter's successor. This is actually a very rare event that may only occur once or twice in a century in our modern times. Many popes never use this authority at all. When it is used, it simply means that a particular doctrine is defined "without error" under the protection of the Holy Spirit. That's it. It means no more and no less than that. Catholics are

---

66 Catechism of the Catholic Church; paragraphs 751 & 877

67 Catechism of the Catholic Church; paragraphs 881 & 891

obliged to believe the pope has settled the matter (without error) by the protection of the Holy Spirit, under the authority given to Saint Peter and his successors by Jesus Christ himself.

CHAPTER NINE
CONCLUSION

I think it's appropriate here to express my gratitude toward the Christians in the Ozarks who have courteously (and sometimes not so courteously) posed these questions to me. While some Catholics may find these questions intimidating, I see them as a grand opportunity. I have never taken offence to them, because you see, as a former Evangelical, I too used to ask these same questions myself. Sadly, when I asked them, all those years ago, I sometimes tended to lean toward the "not so courteous" method. So in other words; I get it. I know how these good folks feel about these issues because I used to feel the exact same way.

I must confess here that I have an admiration for Protestants, especially those of the Baptist, Pentecostal and Evangelical persuasion, and I'm not just saying that because I used to be one. Though I must admit that having been a Baptist, and an Evangelical, has given me insight into what it's like. This inside experience has only caused me to admire them all the more. For Protestants reading this book, I have no criticism. You are my Christian brethren, regardless if you accept me as yours. The Catholic Church embraces you as our Christian brethren and this is taught in the Catechism – no strings attached.[68]

It is the Protestant fire and zeal I admire, as well as the Protestant passion for learning the Scriptures. You see, Protestant Christians have a lot less at their disposal from a Catholic point of view. They don't have all the sacraments, and they are especially lacking the Holy Eucharist. They don't have authentic holy orders backed by apostolic succession. They don't have the wonderful apostolic traditions that complement Biblical teaching. They don't even have all of the Bible! Nor do they have an infallible authority

---

68 Catechism of the Catholic Church; paragraphs 818 & 1271

structure to rely on when doctrinal disputes arise. (This of course has led to numerous divisions within their ranks.) Yet, in spite of this, these people have such a passion for Christ, and his written word, that it always leaves me impressed. It's a testimony of how God (the Holy Spirit) works in people's lives, regardless of the circumstances or lack of resources. Catholics could definitely learn a thing or two from these good folks. For if we Catholics have the same passion and zeal, a love for learning, combined with our sacraments and traditions, we can change the world! We've done it a few times in history already. There is no reason why we can't do it again.

We Catholics should be patient with Protestants as well. They are, whether anyone realises it or not, the future of the Catholic Church in the United States. Baptist, Pentecostal and Evangelical Protestants are converting to Catholicism in increasingly large numbers. Let us also not forget the traditional Anglicans who, through the pope's personal ordinariate for Anglicans, are opening the door of the Catholic Church to what is left of classical Protestantism.

In case you haven't figured it out yet, this book isn't just for Protestants. It's for Catholics too. Because you see there is no reason for Catholics to ever be intimidated, or feel hostile toward, those who pose the kind of questions dealt with herein, either in a genuinely inquisitive way, or in a confrontational way. The purpose of this book is not to be confrontational in return, and I would never recommend arguing with a Protestant over religion. Should we Catholics converse with them? Yes. Should we Catholics attempt to educate them about Catholicism? Yes! Should we Catholics argue with them? No. I wouldn't even recommend debating with them. Winning debates does not win converts. I've never seen it happen, and this is true for both sides. This book is not intended in any way to demean or belittle those who ask such challenging questions of our Catholic faith. On the contrary; were it not for such wonderful questions, there might not exist such a grand opportunity to present an explanation for our Catholic beliefs and traditions. The chance to explain not only helps others understand, but also refreshes our own understanding, and ultimately renews our faith.

That being said I encourage an attitude of reckless cheer for Catholic readers of this book. Not only do we have nothing to be ashamed of as Catholics, but we also have nothing to be confrontational over. Ours is not only the largest Church in the world, but it is even the largest Church in the United States. One might never know that living in the Bible Belt, but it's true. Our faith is what it is, and it was here long before any of these new churches were around to question our legitimacy. Guess what! Our Catholic Christian faith will still be here long after they are gone. Over the last five-hundred years, the Catholic Church has witnessed no less than a dozen Protestant denominations comes and go. In recent decades we have watched many mainline Protestant denominations crumble before our eyes, only to make way for the rise of Evangelical mega-churches. It's all very cyclic you see. These too will come and go, but the Catholic Church will remain just as she always has, because it is the only one established by Jesus Christ on Saint Peter the rock!

As you can see, Catholics have good reasons for believing what we do, and the Catholic Church really is based on sound Biblical teaching. (Though we could just as easily say that the Bible itself is based on sound Catholic teaching.) Many Protestants have converted to Catholicism in recent years, and in many cases this is for profound Biblical reasons. Such was the case with my wife and I after intense prayer and study. Other Protestants have not converted of course, even after studying the Biblical arguments for Catholicism, but as a result of this study, they have been able to put away old fears and superstitions regarding the Catholic Church. In many ways Catholics were the first "Bible Christians" and remain as such today, so it is fitting that we should make our home in America's Bible Belt and flourish here.

RESOURCES

1. Bible, Douay-Rheims, American Edition, 1899

2. Bible, Revised Standard Version – Catholic Edition, 1965, 1966

3. Bible, King James Version 1611

4. Catechism of the Catholic Church, Second Edition, Doubleday Publishing, 1997

5. Code of Canon Law, Vatican Online Archives, 1983, http://www.vatican.va/archive/ENG1104/_INDEX.HTM

6. Sacerdotalis coelibatus, Vatican Online Archives, 1967, http://www.vatican.va/holy_father/paul_vi/encyclicals/docume nts/hf_p-vi_enc_24061967_sacerdotalis_en.html

7. Anglicanorum coetibus, Vatican Online Archives, 2009, http://www.vatican.va/holy_father/benedict_xvi/apost_constitu tions/documents/hf_ben-xvi_apc_20091104_anglicanorum-coetibus_en.html

8. Charol Shakeshaft, *Educator Sexual Misconduct Report*, U.S. Department of Education, Office of the Under Secretary, 2004 http://www2.ed.gov/rschstat/research/pubs/misconductreview /report.pdf

9. Justin Martyr, *First Apology*, circa 155 AD

10. Ignatius of Antioch, *Epistle to the Smyrnaeans*, circa 105 AD

11. Ignatius of Antioch, *Epistle to the Romans*, circa 105 AD

12. Clement of Rome, *The First Epistle of Clement*, circa 96 AD

13. Irenaeus, *Against Heresies*, circa 180 AD

14. Eusebius, *Church History*, circa 325 AD

15. Epiphanius, *Panarion*, circa 377 AD

16. Tertullian, *Against Marcion*, circa 210 AD

17. Tertullian, *Scorpiace*, circa 212 AD

18. Peter of Alexandria, *The Canonical Epistle*, circa 306 AD

19. Cyril of Jerusalem, *Catechetical Lectures*, circa 350 AD

20. Thirty-Nine Articles of Religion, 1563

21. Westminster Confession of Faith 1647

22. Brief Statement of the Doctrinal Position of the Missouri Synod, Adopted 1932

23. Pope John Paul II, speech to bishops of Southern Germany, Dec. 4, 1992

24. Pope Benedict XVI, Angelus, Vatican City, 26 February 2012

25. Fr. Mario P. Romero, *Unabridged Christianity*, Queenship Publishing Company, 1999

26. Taylor R. Marshall, *The Crucified Rabbi*, Saint John Press, 2009

27. Scott Hahn, *The Lamb's Supper*, Doubleday Religion, 1999

28. Stephen K. Ray, *Crossing The Tiber*, Ignatius Press, 1997

CPSIA information can be obtained
at www.ICGtesting.com
Printed in the USA
LVOW12s1301250416

485204LV00006B/252/P